Values Education
Rationale, Strategies, and Procedures

Edited by Lawrence E. Metcalf

Consultant
Roland Payette

Contributors
G. Gary Casper
James Chadwick
Jerrold R. Coombs
Milton O. Meux

41st Yearbook, 1971

NATIONAL COUNCIL FOR THE SOCIAL STUDIES
A National Affiliate of the National Education Association
1201 Sixteenth Street, N.W., Washington, D.C. 20036
Price: Paperbound $5.00; Clothbound $6.50

The National Council for the Social Studies is a National Affiliate of the National Education Association of the United States. It is the professional organization of educators at all levels — elementary, secondary, college, and university — who are interested in the teaching of social studies. Membership in the National Council for the Social Studies includes a subscription to the Council's official journal, SOCIAL EDUCATION, and a copy of the Yearbook. In addition, the Council publishes bulletins, curriculum studies, pamphlets, and other materials of practical use for teachers of the social studies. Membership dues are $12.00 a year. Applications for membership and orders for the purchase of publications should be sent to the Executive Secretary, 1201 Sixteenth Street, N.W., Washington, D.C. 20036.

Preface

☐ In the spring of 1970 on a small college campus in the West a group of students ran the American flag up a pole upside down. Another group objected and one of its members climbed the pole and brought the flag down. This precipitated a major altercation, and in the melee that followed, the flag was torn apart and local police had to be called to quell the disturbance. Although these young people were living in the year 1970 and had the advantage of thirteen to sixteen years of formal education, their ability to resolve value conflicts was evidently little better than that of their forebears who inhabited the earth many thousands of years ago—long before there were schools and formal education, to say nothing of social studies education.

It seems incredible that man has made so little headway in values education and conflict resolution considering the amount of attention that has been given to these matters through the years. All of the world's major religions concern themselves with values development. The writings of philosophers, poets, and playwrights are almost entirely values-based. Every society has established ideas about rightness and wrongness and devises ways to instill those values in its young and ways to enforce behavior codes based on those values. Almost without exception societies today, as they have for thousands of years, embrace a system of values that rejects killing, stealing, lying, and cheating. But men everywhere keep on killing, stealing, lying, and cheating. One can hardly believe that our own nation, which embraces and even demonstrates humanitarian values in so many ways, actually mass produces bullets, rifles, mortars, artillery, aircraft, and bombs designed specifically to kill human beings. Moreover, it maintains expensive and sophisticated training programs to prepare its men to do the killing. Thus, while we invest a million dollars on cancer research presumably to preserve human life, we spend billions on systems designed to destroy life. The same policeman who will risk a bone-breaking fall to rescue a stranded kitten on a rooftop will shoot and kill a fleeing burglar. The same society that becomes incensed over the killing of baby seals for their pelts seems unconcerned about living hells called prisons or, even more ironically, "correctional institutions." The same community that is aroused over the spread of venereal disease among its young will not allow sex education in its school curriculum. The same citizen who proudly carries the flag as a patriotic gesture in the Fourth of July parade later in the week in the barber shop voices his views regarding what should be done with those who engage in protests: "Shoot the bastards!"

Thus we are brought to the profound enigma of the creature called "man." Why is it that our behavior individually and collectively is often inconsistent, or even contrary, to the values we profess? Is man by nature simply a scoundrel who cannot or will not conduct his life in accordance with humanitarian values? Or is man an inept learner when it comes to values education? Did man develop differentially, with his cognitive powers developing much more rapidly than his capacity to cope with corresponding value conflicts? Or have the exhortative strategies used to teach values through the thousands of years of man's history been inadequate or ineffective?

Among the recent finds in the archaeological diggings in Africa was a human skull crushed in a way to suggest that this man of antiquity had fallen victim to the evil ways of his fellow man. The same thing could happen and does happen almost any night in any of the large cities of this nation today. Surely a nation that can send men to the moon and return them safely should have the capacity to teach its people how to resolve value conflicts in more acceptable ways than crushing each other's skulls—either psychologically or literally.

The time is overdue when an all-out effort must be made to find productive approaches to values education and conflict resolution. This yearbook, *Values Education: Rationale, Strategies, and Procedures,* is a step in that direction. Professor Metcalf in his Introduction cautions the reader that he may find it hard going. This is as it should be, for we are dealing with an incredibly complex subject. If the problem were an easy one, man would have solved it long ago. Too frequently simplistic proposals have been advanced as strategies for values education.

The National Council for the Social Studies expresses its thanks and appreciation to Professor Lawrence E. Metcalf and his colleagues, Gary Casper, James Chadwick, Jerrold Coombs, Milton Meux, and Roland Payette, for the preparation of this thoughtful yearbook.

JOHN JAROLIMEK, *President*
National Council for the Social Studies

Acknowledgments

We gratefully acknowledge the assistance of Terry Applegate and Keith Evans, who helped with drafts of the chapters and participated in one of the conflict resolutions, and to Janet Clayton for participating in the other conflict resolution. We would also like to acknowledge the assistance of the secretarial staff of the Bureau of Educational Research of the University of Utah: Linda Andrew, Barbara Tomita, Janice Tsujimoto, and especially to Becky Lange for her invaluable help at many crucial moments.

Members of the Committee
G. Gary Casper
James Chadwick
Jerrold Coombs
Lawrence E. Metcalf
Milton Meux
Roland Payette

Introduction

□ I want to say a few words about this yearbook, how it happened to be written, what it attempts to do, and to what uses a teacher or methods instructor might put it. A few years ago I was asked by the Publications Committee of the National Council for the Social Studies to assume the responsibility for developing and editing a yearbook on values education. I was most happy to accept this assignment. For a good many years I had made the study of values education one of my chief professional concerns. But I was not at all certain as to what kind of yearbook NCSS should attempt to develop.

I had only a few very general ideas. The yearbook should attempt to help teachers with their problems in values education, and it should attempt to help all teachers — elementary, junior and senior high school, junior college, and last but not least, college teachers of methods and curriculum. Another general idea had to do with the dualism between cognitive and affective domains. No teacher ever works in one of these domains to the exclusion of the other, and it would be misleading for any yearbook to imply that such separation is either desirable or possible. It therefore seemed to me that the yearbook might have a heavy emphasis upon logic and rationality as means by which to apply cognitive content to the affective domain. Just how this might be done I was not at all sure.

A third general idea was that although questions of truth are logically distinct from questions of value, one ought not to pursue objectives in values education that are in conflict with the cognitive purposes of schools. Many teachers are caught up in a conflict between a desire to teach thinking and knowledge, and a desire to teach certain attitudes. Drug education, anticommunist education, black studies — these are only a few of the areas in which such conflict may be manifest. Black educators have pointed to the biased practices of white history. Some have gone so far as to claim that objectivity is a myth. I suppose that the most outstanding example of distortion has been our programs in anticommunist education. Many schools have suppressed information about communism if in the judgment of the school authorities such information might place communism in a favorable light. This kind of practice, in addition to being unnecessary, is plainly dishonest. One of the ironies of education is the extent to which some teachers believe that the practice of dishonesty is necessary to the teaching of honest patriotism! More to the point, such practice violates the principle of academic freedom. We cannot have academic freedom except as teachers make responsible use of that freedom. There is nothing more irresponsible in the field of ideas than the suppression of evidence in the name of attitude or values education. Many of our current attempts to teach students "proper attitudes" toward taking or using drugs reflect this conflict between truth and honesty on the one hand, and inculcation of attitudes and values on the other.[1]

A fourth general idea related value education to some of the developments that are now called "the new social studies." We do not have complete agreement on what this expression means. But there is general agreement that whatever its precise meaning it does mean in general a cognitively tougher content that places heavy logical demands upon both teachers and students. This development in content selection is consistent with another current emphasis, the concern at the research level with the logical problems or aspects of instruction. This research has helped us all to see that a description is not an explanation, that a concept is not an empirical generalization, that an attitude is not the same as a value judgment, and finally, that some theories are testable while others are not, and that a tested and confirmed theory is the most useful "fact" that anyone might teach. Each kind of content — conceptual, empirical, theoretical, and valuational — has its own internal logic. We use facts in order to "test" our concepts, generalizations, values, and theories but in each case the role of facts is somewhat different because the internal

---

[1] For an excellent discussion of the problems of drug education, see Seymour Halleck, "The Great Drug Education Hoax," *The Progressive*, July, 1970, pp. 30-33.

logic is different. One of the most interesting and significant features of valuational content is that it brings together in a functional sense our understanding of different kinds of content and their internal logics. For purposes of learning how to deal with the new and tough content of the new social studies nothing could be more ideal than a yearbook on values education that would apply to classroom practice our emergent knowledge on the logic of teaching.

And this brings us to a fifth general idea. Because the knowledge on the logic of teaching is not yet well established, and like most emergent knowledge not entirely clear, any yearbook that would take such knowledge seriously would have to have an experimental posture, or outlook. It would have to encourage teachers to experiment with a set of procedures and strategies for which a rationale had been provided. Action research in the classroom with or without the collaboration of "university experts" appeared to be one of the desired effects of a yearbook in values education.

And, finally, it was one of my very general ideas that the yearbook should come to terms with the current cry for relevance. War, ecology, alienation, pollution, racism, black studies, the military-industrial complex, hippies, drop-outs, cop-outs, student activism, both protest and disruption — all these topics and concerns deserved and demanded recognition in a yearbook on values education. But it had to be the kind of recognition of the cry for relevance that would not do violence to knowledge, logic, or academic freedom. Such recognition would have to reject any concept of relevance that would assume that either truth or morality is that which corresponds with the feelings of students. It would not reject objectivity as a myth nor would it pander to the impulses of turned-on youth. At the same time, it would constructively aid students in their efforts to define and locate their preferred worlds.

How The Yearbook Was Written

With these general ideas in mind I next sought help from a number of colleagues in education. I was able to find a group of like-minded young professors who had a clear concept of rational or logical value education with which they had been experimenting over a number of years. My discussions with these young men convinced me that we would have to write a book rather than a yearbook. It would be a book that would have internal unity with a development of ideas from chapter to chapter. It would call for very close collaboration among the several authors. In a sense, all NCSS yearbooks have demanded and reflected a degree of collaboration from the authors. But the kind of yearbook in value education that emerged from our discussions rejected eclecticism, or a collage of discretely different chapters written by many and different authors with little or no bridge or footpath running from chapter to chapter. Of course, any rejection of eclecticism risks the charge of bias and dogmatism, and we have tried to avoid this trap by casting our proposal in an experimental light.

The product that emerged from this thinking has a number of features. First, the yearbook is short. It does not take long to develop a single idea or hypothesis. We think the hypothesis is clear enough to be experimented with. We do not know for sure what difficulties teachers will encounter, or what results they will obtain. But the idea here presented is promising enough to try out in classrooms. Second, the yearbook is difficult. This is often the case with short books addressed to development of a testable hypothesis. It is a book that will have to be studied. It will have to be read and reread, and it can't really be understood except as its readers try out its ideas in some kind of instructional context. Third, the number of writers or contributors is small. Many times we were tempted to invite other contributors, and thereby expand upon the scope of value education. In each case, we resisted the temptation because we did not want to risk destruction of the book's internal unity. Consequently, many eminent thinkers in the field of value education may feel slighted because they were not asked to contribute. Their absence from the yearbook is no criticism of their competence. We hope to receive their contributions in the form of critical and constructive response. We make no claim to having all the answers. We do not even claim to have in our possession a finished or polished program. We have nothing to offer but a hypothesis, and publication by NCSS constitutes no endorsement of the program. All that publication by NCSS endorses is a climate of experimentation, and the kind of experimentation that enlists the participatory investigation of classroom teachers. We do not get experimentation from any group by exhorting it to experiment. Openmindedness is not created by pleas to be critical, open, and experimental. It is the slow, detailed, and deliberate explication of a hypothesis so that teachers are in a position to try out something that is detailed and comprehensive that is more likely to create open and inquiring classrooms. This is all that we have attempted to do.

LAWRENCE E. METCALF, *Editor*

University of Illinois, Urbana
June 1971

The Authors

CASPER, G. GARY. Assistant Professor of Data Processing at Weber State College. He received his M.S. in Educational Psychology from the University of Utah, where he is currently completing work on a Ph.D. program. He has worked with Milton Meux and James Chadwick developing and testing procedures and materials based upon the approach to value problems in the Social Studies described in this yearbook. He has authored articles in the field of Data Processing and is currently interested in the implications and application of computer technology to education. Other interests include counseling and the resolution of value conflicts in small groups. He holds membership in the Data Processing Management Association.

CHADWICK, JAMES. Ed.D. in Educational Administration from the University of Utah. He had several years experience teaching in the public schools in both junior high and senior high, with emphasis on the Social Studies. After receiving his doctorate he became vice-president of The Citadel Enterprises and a member of the board of directors of Capital Leasing. He returned to education as Title III coordinator of the State of Utah. He is presently Needs Assessment Specialist and Dissemination Specialist in the Division of Research and Innovation of the Utah State Board of Education. His present interest is in continued research on procedures for value analysis, especially the implications of the procedures for community involvement in the Social Studies, the resolution of value conflicts, and ego development.

COOMBS, JERROLD. Professor of Philosophy of Education at the University of British Columbia. He received his Ph.D. in Philosophy of Education from the University of Illinois, where he worked with B. Othanel Smith and Milton Meux in studying the logical dimension of classroom behavior and teaching strategy. His publications include articles on teaching, indoctrination, and equality in education. Currently he is pursuing research in the areas of moral education and concept teaching strategies.

METCALF, LAWRENCE E. Ph.D., Ohio State University, 1948. Professor of Social Studies Education, University of Illinois, since 1949. Prior to that time he taught in the public schools of Ohio, Goddard College in Vermont, and the University of Georgia. He has also taught at numerous universities during summer sessions. In 1955 he coauthored with Maurice P. Hunt a landmark publication in social studies education entitled *Teaching High School Social Studies*. A second edition appeared in 1968. A former member of the Board of Directors of the National Council for the Social Studies, he has written numerous journal articles, and has served as an educational consultant to a number of national curriculum projects. Currently, he is consultant to the curriculum and teacher education projects of the World Law Fund.

MEUX, MILTON. Ph.D. in Psychology from the University of Illinois, and currently Associate Professor of Educational Psychology at the University of Utah. He worked at the University of Illinois with B. Othanel Smith and Jerrold Coombs developing two classroom observation systems, one for the logical and the other for the strategic aspects of teaching, and a theory of teaching as rule-guided behavior. He is author of a variety of articles on classroom observation systems and value models, and coauthor of *A Study of the Logic of Teaching*. In addition to value problems in the Social Studies, his current interests are in the resolution of value conflicts in small groups, value problems in psychological research, and theoretical and philosophical problems in psychology. He is a member of a number of professional societies, including the American Psychological Association, American Educational Research Association, Society for the Psychological Study of Social Issues, and American Society for Value Inquiry.

Consultant: PAYETTE, ROLAND F. is Associate Professor of Education, University of Illinois, Urbana. He has been a secondary school teacher of social studies and a director of curriculum and research in the public schools. He was a test specialist at Educational Testing Service and has written numerous government and social studies tests for E.T.S. and for Science Research Associates.

Contents

1

Objectives
of Value Analysis

JERROLD R. COOMBS

☐ Having students analyse, discuss, and decide value questions, particularly those about which there is public controversy, has recently become the subject of renewed concern among social studies teachers. Despite their concern, many teachers cannot operate effectively in this area because of confusion and uncertainty. They are confused as to what, if any, legitimate educational objectives are to be obtained by such value analysis. This in turn produces uncertainty about procedures to be used by the teacher in directing value analyses, and about the means of evaluating student achievement resulting from such exercises. The purpose of this chapter is to make a start at clarifying the objectives of value analysis.

Some Preliminary Clarification

If we are to become clear about objectives, we must begin by being clear about the terms we use in talking about value analysis, particularly the term "value." Very often the term "value" is used in such a way as to be ambiguous. For example, in some contexts it may refer either to the things people hold to be of worth or to the standards by which people judge the worth of things. To avoid confusion we will use the term only in the phrase "value judgments." Value judgments may be defined roughly as those judgments which rate things with respect to their worth. The following statements express value judgments.

1. Nixon is a good president.

2. Washington is a beautiful city.

3. Capitalism is an efficient economic system.

4. War is mass murder.

5. The sinking of the *Titanic* was a disaster.

6. Proportional representation is an adequate way of giving voice to the will of the people.

7. The U.S. ought to stop testing nuclear weapons.

8. Presidents should be elected by direct popular vote.

Words such as "good," "beautiful," "efficient," "murder" are called "evaluative terms" or "rating terms" because they are commonly used to rate things with respect to their worth. The terms "ought" and "should" are also evaluative terms when they are used in prescriptive statements, i.e., statements telling us what to do. Such statements can be translated into statements containing more obvious evaluative terms. If some action ought to be taken or should be taken, then it is either right or desirable to take the action.

We will refer to the thing being rated in the value judgment as the "value object." Almost any sort of thing can be a value object. We evaluate physical objects, events, people, actions, institutions, and practices as well as classes of such things. In the statements above, Nixon, Washington, capitalism, war, sinking of the *Titanic,* proportional representation, testing nuclear weapons, and direct popular election of presidents are all value objects.

Value judgments may contain positive evaluations, negative evaluations, or neutral evaluations. For example, statements 1 and 2 express positive evaluations, statements 4, and 5 express negative evaluations, and statement 6 expresses a neutral evaluation. A positive evaluation places the value object high on some scale of worth, a negative evaluation places it low, and a neutral evaluation places it around the midpoint.

Evaluative terms vary with respect to how much they tell us about the value objects to which they are applied. Some evaluative terms such as "good" and "bad" tell us nothing definite about the characteristics of value objects, while other terms such as "murder" give us quite a bit of information. The judgment that Nixon is a good president tells us nothing definite about President Nixon. But the judgment that war is mass murder does tell us something about war, namely that it entails deliberate killing on a large scale.

One other feature of value judgments is worthy of mention. There are several different points of view according to which we assess value objects. We may assess a value object from an aesthetic, a moral, an economic, or a prudential point of view. Other points of view can be identified, but these are the most important.[1] In addition, we may make an overall judgment of the worth of the value object, taking into account various points of view. Some evaluative terms ordinarily are used to make assessments from only one point of view. For example, "beautiful" and "ugly" ordinarily rate things from an aesthetic point of view. "Efficient" rates things from an economic point of view. "Immoral" rates things from a moral point of view, and "wise" conveys a prudential rating. Most evaluative terms can be used with reference to more than one point of view. "Good," "bad," "desirable," and "undesirable" can be used to rate things from virtually any point of view. We shall have more to say about the various points of view in a later section of this chapter. We will be particularly concerned with the moral point of view since it is the one which causes most confusion.

Value judgments are diverse and complex, having many guises and many functions. What has been said so far is not meant to be an exhaustive portrayal of such judgments. However, it should help us avoid confusion in discussing the objectives of value analysis.

Relevance of the Logic of Justification

Discussions of value analysis in an educational context suggest at least four possible objectives of such an enterprise.

1. To teach students that some value object is to be given a particular rating; to teach, for example, that the U.N. is a good thing or that premarital sex is wrong. This sort of objective is what people appear to have in mind when they advocate teaching values or teaching citizenship.

2. To help each student make the most rational, defensible value judgment he can make about the value object in question.

3. To equip students with the capacity and inclination to make rational, defensible value judgments.

4. To teach students how to operate as members of a group attempting to come to a common value judgment about some value object.

Teachers have to determine which, if any, of these proposed objectives are defensible educational goals. This implies that they also must know with some specificity just what they are attempting to accomplish in each case. What exactly is one attempting to accomplish when he sets out to teach students to make rational value judgments? When teachers are clearer about these things, they should be in a much better position to consider the kinds of procedures they should use in promoting and guiding value deliberations. Of course, having a clear understanding of one's goals is not a sufficient basis for determining what teaching procedures to use. It is necessary as well to have empirical knowledge indicating the kinds of procedures which are likely to produce the results we want. Chapter Two of this yearbook will attempt to assess the current state of the relevant empirical knowledge.

In claiming that teachers have to determine which goals of value analysis are legitimate, I do not mean to imply that teachers should be the final arbiters of educational goals. While

I do not wish to argue the point here, my own view is that, in the final analysis, the authority for such decisions should rest with the community served by the educational institution. But, the community, aside from a few vocal minority groups, does not make clear in any detail what it expects of the schools. This means that, like it or not, teachers must make decisions about goals. However, they must have good grounds for their decisions, and they must be prepared to justify them to the community.

It is unlikely that teachers could come to well-founded decisions about the objectives of value analysis without some understanding of the nature of value judgments and the way in which they are justified. Consider the first objective on the list above, namely the objective of teaching particular value conclusions. If value judgments can be shown to be true or false in the same manner as judgments about matters of fact, a strong defense for adopting this goal is at hand. We can offer the same grounds for teaching a particular value conclusion as for teaching a factual conclusion, namely that it is true and important. However, if evaluative judgments are, as some have claimed, merely expressions of emotions, preferences, attitudes, or tastes, we shall need a different sort of justification for teaching particular value conclusions. Indeed, we may find no justification for adopting this sort of objective for value analysis. Notice also that the third objective on the list, that of teaching students to make rational value judgments, is defensible only if the nature of value judgments is such that it makes sense to regard them as rational or irrational.

Understanding something of the logic of justifying value judgments is important as well in becoming clear about what exactly is implied by each of the proposed objectives. For example, the objective of teaching students to make rational value judgments implies that we will teach them to follow some standards of rationality in their judgments. Thus getting clear in detail about this objective is dependent in part on getting clear in detail about the standards of rationality applicable to value judgments.

Although clarifying the nature and justification of value judgments is an important first step in unravelling the confusion and uncertainty surrounding the objectives of value analysis, it is by no means an easy job. Many very good philosophers have been working on this task over a period of hundreds of years. Still there are things about value judgments which we do not know or cannot agree upon. What I shall have to say on this matter is neither new nor original. My justification for saying it here is that to my knowledge there is no single work which covers all the things that need to be said in a manner which is concise, intelligible to non-philosophers, and directly relevant to the problem of clarifying objectives of value deliberation. While these views are not entirely non-controversial, they are supported by arguments which I consider compelling.* The reader is not asked to accept the conclusions on anyone's authority, but rather on the basis of the arguments offered in support of them. Because the arguments presented here are of necessity brief, a selected bibliography is provided at the end of this chapter for those who wish to delve more deeply into the issues.

Some people hold the view that any assertions about the nature of value judgments and how they are justified must themselves be value assertions expressing the author's basic values. Thus they contend that no account of justification is free of presuppositions themselves requiring justification. While there is a grain of truth in this view, in the main it is mistaken. It is possible, though difficult, to describe how we justify value decisions without thereby making any value assertions. This is what the present discussion will attempt. Briefly, what we want to uncover are the rules which govern our reasoning about value questions. Thus our inquiry is similar to that of the philosopher of science who attempts to map the rules governing our reasoning about empirical matters. However, as Paul Taylor points out, we are not concerned merely with describing how the majority of people

---

* Some issues regarding the nature of value judgments are still *very* controversial. No attempt is made here to resolve all such issues.

make and justify value decisions. A great many people, perhaps most, do not always think rigorously in making value decisions. Consequently, we want to find out what rules people follow when they are aware of how they are reasoning and are satisfied with it.[2] In a sense, then, we want to find out the rules which govern satisfactory or rational reasoning in the realm of making and justifying value judgments. "Rational" here means that manner of operating which one accepts when he has full knowledge of what he is doing. It is important to be clear that we are not *proposing* canons of rationality for reasoning about value matters. We are attempting to make explicit the ideal of rationality implicit in our use of value language.

Value Judgments and Factual Judgments

There are several widely held views about the nature of value judgments. Since it is likely that many teachers hold one or another of these views, it may be well to begin our discussion by considering these popular conceptions. One such conception holds that statements expressing value judgments are not significantly different from factual statements. The two types of statements may be shown to be true or false in the same way. This view has a certain amount of face validity. Value statements, like factual statements, appear to tell us something about the world of experience, and it seems sensible to assert that they are true or false.

The deficiencies of this view begin to show when we attempt to verify value statements by means of the procedures used in verifying factual statements. These verification procedures are of three types, designated here as VP1, VP2, and VP3.

VP1 is used only when the statement to be verified is an observation statement, i.e., when it reports a particular observable condition. The procedure consists in making an observation to find out if the condition reported in the statement is present. Using this procedure one might verify the statement "There is a pen on my desk" by looking or feeling on my desk to find out if there is a pen on it.

VP2 is the procedure of verifying a factual statement by deducing it from other true factual statements. If a statement can be shown to be the conclusion of a valid deductive argument having true premises, the statement must be true. For example, we might attempt to verify the statement "This vase is 2000 years old" by showing it to be the conclusion of an argument with the following premises. Artifacts with chemical property X are 2000 years old. This vase has chemical property X. Since this is a valid argument, the conclusion would have to be regarded as true if the premises were true. A second version of VP2 allows definitions as well as factual statements in the premises. In this version we might verify a statement such as "X is fragile" by deducing it from true factual statements about X plus a definition of the term "fragile."

VP3 is used to verify generalizations and involves two steps. First a statement of some observable condition is deduced from the generalization in conjunction with other known facts. Then observations are made to determine whether or not this predicted condition obtains. The presence of the predicted condition provides evidence confirming the truth of the generalization. The absence of the predicted condition serves to falsify the generalization.

The question now to be settled is whether or not value statements can be justified in any of these three ways. Are value statements rating the worth of single objects, events, etc. capable of verification by means of VP1? Consider the value statement "That is a good car." Can this statement be verified by making observations of the car in question to determine if some condition reported in the statement is present? If we examine a car we observe color, size, shape, amount of gas used, stopping distance, etc. What we do not see is the goodness of the car. Nor do we taste, smell, hear, or feel it. We may *decide* on the basis of our observations that the car is good, but we do not observe goodness.

Were it the case that goodness could be observed, it would not be possible for two persons, both of whom had thoroughly tested and examined the car, to disagree as to whether or not the car is good. But in fact such a disagreement is not only possible, it is a common occurrence. Indeed it is a general feature of evaluative reasoning that persons can and do make contrary evaluations about objects and events even when they have made the same observations.

In sum, value assertions do not merely report or describe observable conditions, and they cannot be verified by means of VP1.

Putting aside consideration of VP2 temporarily, let us see whether or not VP3 can do the job of verifying general value statements. It can do the job only if it is possible to deduce from the evaluative statement in conjunction with true factual statements a statement describing observable phenomena. In the case of many general evaluative statements such a deduction is clearly not possible. Consider the value statement "Fighting is bad." This statement in conjunction with the factual statement "X is fighting" implies "X is bad." But "X is bad" does not describe observable phenomena. This case illustrates a significant point about a large class of value assertions. The only inference from this sort of general value assertion that is logically relevant to verifying the assertion is a value statement; a statement which does not describe observable phenomena. Therefore, many evaluative statements cannot be verified by means of VP3.*

Many people hold the view that value assertions can be verified by means of VP2. The attraction of this view stems from the fact that in some sense we do derive our value conclusions from factual considerations. In a previous example we noted that we cannot observe the goodness of a car, but it does seem that we conclude that a car is good on the basis of facts we know about the car. Indeed, though this is letting the

---

* Some singular value assertions can be shown to be *false* by VP1, and some general value assertions can be shown to be *false* by VP3. This applies only to those assertions containing rating terms such as "murder" which give information about characteristics of the value object. It does not apply to evaluations using primary rating terms such as "good," "bad," "right," "wrong," "ought," etc. *No* value statement can be shown to be true by VP1 and *no* general value statement can be significantly confirmed by VP3.

cat out of the bag prematurely, the whole task of clarifying the nature of value judgments is to describe exactly how we reason from facts to value conclusions.

There are, you will remember, two versions of VP2: (1) deducing the statement to be verified from true factual statements and (2) deducing the statement to be verified from true factual statements and definitions. The first version can be used to verify statements only if it is possible to construct a *valid deductive* argument having only factual statements as premises and an evaluative statement as a conclusion. No such argument has yet been constructed.* The second version of VP2 can do the job of verifying value statements only if it is possible to define evaluative terms accurately by means of a definition itself containing no evaluative terms. No such definition has yet been produced.

There are good grounds for believing that the kinds of arguments and definitions which would allow us to use VP2 in verifying value statements are not possible. They are not possible because evaluative assertions serve functions not served by factual assertions. Evaluative assertions serve to tell us what to do; they provide guidance as to how persons are to act, choose, or feel about something. Factual assertions by themselves do not perform these functions. Thus definitions which permit the translation of value assertions into factual assertions cannot be accurate. And since the conclusion of a valid deductive argument asserts nothing that is not implied in the premises, arguments from factual assertions to evaluative conclusions cannot be valid.

Value Judgments and Attitudes

A second widely held but inadequate view of value judgments may be characterized as follows. An evaluative statement is merely an expression or indication of the attitude or feeling of the person making the statement. If one says that

---

* Arguments of this type are often persuasive, but they are not valid unless some value assertion is added to the premises. They persuade us because we accept the suppressed (unstated) value premise.

medicare is a good thing, he is merely expressing his attitude of liking, approving, or being favorably disposed toward medicare. Further, it does not make sense to consider attitudes as being true or false, correct or incorrect, justified or unjustified. We can justify beliefs or show them to be correct by citing relevant facts which serve as evidence for the beliefs. We cannot give facts to show that attitudes or feelings are correct or justified. What facts, for instance, could show that it is correct to dislike blondes or that one is justified in enjoying football? Since evaluative statements are merely expressions of attitudes we only delude ourselves if we think they can be shown to be correct or justified. True, we do engage in arguments which purport to justify our evaluative assertions. But the only real purpose these arguments serve is to persuade others to adopt the same attitude we have.

This point of view has an element of truth in it, but it is faulty in several important respects. It is true that evaluative assertions imply that the person making the assertion has a certain attitude. If I say that school desegregation is a good thing, I am indicating that I have a positive or approving attitude toward school desegregation. It is also true that arguments given in support of my evaluation serve to persuade others to adopt my positive attitude or to persuade me to maintain my positive attitude. The deficiencies of this view lie in the conclusions that evaluative assertions are *merely* expressions of attitudes, and arguments supporting evaluations are *only* attempts to persuade people to adopt a given attitude.

It is easy to show that evaluative assertions are not merely expressions of attitudes. We do not make the same kind of investigation in deciding whether or not to accept or believe an evaluative assertion as we do in deciding whether or not to accept an expression of attitude.

Consider the following sentences.

1. U.S. involvement in the Vietnamese war is wrong.

2. I disapprove of U.S. involvement in the Vietnamese war.

Sentence #1 is an evaluative statement; sentence #2 is an

expression of attitude. To determine the acceptability of the first sentence we would gather information about the U.S. involvement in Vietnam and its consequences. The acceptability of the second statement is not decided in the same way. Rather, we would attempt to assure ourselves that the speaker was not deceiving us about his attitudes or feelings concerning Vietnam.

The view that arguments given to support evaluations are only attempts to persuade persons to adopt a given attitude has several weaknesses. First, it is wrong in assuming that attitudes cannot be justified. We can and do give reasons to justify attitudes. To justify disapproving of U.S. involvement in the Vietnamese war we might give as a reason the fact that it increases the rate of killing in the war. This reason is not meant merely to explain why we have the attitude but to show that the attitude is acceptable.

The second weakness in this view is that it does not allow us to make a very important distinction which we commonly do make in considering evaluative arguments, that is, the distinction between relevant justifying reasons and illegitimate attempts to persuade. In attempting to decide the worth of something we sort out persuasive considerations on the basis of whether they are legitimate and relevant or not. A teacher might want to give a student a good grade because the student is friendly and appealing, but he generally regards these considerations as irrelevant. This distinction between relevant and irrelevant considerations is learned in the act of learning to use value language. When a child states as his reason for hitting someone "I don't like him," we are apt to tell the child "That's no reason for hitting him." Thus we teach him that some considerations are not relevant, i.e., do not count as reasons. Any adequate account of evaluative reasoning must take into account this important distinction.

In sum, the view of evaluative judgments being considered here does not do justice to the fact that evaluative assertions are meant to express *justifiable* attitudes and they are meant to have *legitimate* authority over the conduct and attitudes of others. When we say that space exploration is a good thing, we not only imply that *we* approve of space exploration and that we want others to approve of it; we also imply that there are compelling reasons for *anyone* adopting a positive attitude toward space exploration.

Features of Evaluative Reasoning

It is time now to provide a more positive account of the nature and justification of value judgments. One of the most significant points to note is that it is always relevant to ask for justification of value judgments. That is, it is never beside the point to ask for reasons or grounds for the judgment. If someone asserts that racism is bad, it is relevant to ask why it is bad or what makes it bad. Two sorts of information can be given in response to this question. The evaluator may respond by giving facts about racism in light of which he regards it as bad. He may say, for instance, that racism is bad because it produces needless suffering. Alternatively, the evaluator may answer by citing a value principle such as "It is bad to have people suffer needlessly." A full specification of the reasons for any value judgment contains both facts about the thing being evaluated and rules or criteria which relate the facts to the rating. A person making an evaluation commits himself to having supporting facts because value judgments are logically dependent to a degree on factual considerations. One cannot apply a given rating to one value object and not to another if there is no difference in the facts about the two objects. One cannot, for example, say that table A is good and table B is not good if the two tables are exactly the same. Evaluations can differ only when there are differences in the facts. It must be kept in mind, however, that value judgments are not dependent upon nor derivable from facts alone.

Making a value judgment commits the evaluator to a value principle because his judgment logically implies a principle. If someone says that this pencil is good he commits himself to the value principle that any pencil just like this one is good. It would be logically inconsistent to assert the judgment and deny the value principle. The precise nature of the value principle implied by any judgment is indicated by the facts which are given to support the judgment. Suppose someone says this is a good pencil because it writes smoothly and feels comfortable in my hand. He commits himself to the principle that any pencil which writes smoothly and feels comfortable in my hand is a good pencil. If smoothness and comfort are what make this a good pencil, it follows that any pencil with these same features must be regarded as good.

The value principle implied in any judgment relates the supporting facts to the evaluative term used in making the judgment. In the example above the value principle relates facts about comfort and smoothness to the evaluative term "good."

To summarize, anyone making a value judgment commits himself to: (1) a value principle, and (2) a set of facts about the value object which shows that the principle applies to the value object. The facts and the value principle comprise the premises of a deductive argument having the value judgment as its conclusion.

While the rudiments of evaluative argument described above are rather simple, the actual process of evaluative decision making can be rather complex. We arrive at an evaluation on the basis of relevant facts. To be relevant to a value decision, facts have to meet two conditions: (1) they must be facts about the value object, and (2) they must be facts to which the evaluator ascribes some value rating. If the value decision is being made from a particular point of view, the value rating ascribed to the facts must be from the same point of view. The first condition needs no elaboration. The second condition may be equally obvious to some, but it is deserving of some explanation and illustration. Suppose someone were trying to decide whether or not it is good to build freeways into cities. One of the facts he knows about building freeways into cities is that they increase the total number of cars in the city. Unless the evaluator ascribes some value rating to having more or fewer cars in cities, i.e., thinks it is desirable or undesirable, this fact is not relevant to his evaluative decision.

To have ascribed value to some class of conditions is to have accepted or established a value *criterion*. We begin to accept or establish value criteria from a very early age, and by the time a person enters school he has a very extensive set of such criteria. Some widely held criteria include: it is wrong to cheat, lie, steal, kill, and hurt other people; it is good to keep promises, pay debts, and be healthy. Value criteria do not indicate the way in which a certain type of condition is to be rated in all circumstances. They indicate only how the condition is to be rated in the main or "other things being equal." For example, most of us accept the value criterion that it is wrong to lie. But there are many times when it is right to lie, as when lying will save someone's life or diminish his suffering. Thus while this value criterion does not hold in all cases, it does hold in most cases, or when there are no exceptional circumstances.

Value criteria not only make facts relevant, they give valence to facts. That is, they determine whether the facts support positive or negative evaluations. Suppose I am trying to decide whether euthanasia is good or bad. My value criterion that killing is wrong gives negative valence to the fact that euthanasia involves killing. Thus this fact supports a negative evaluation of euthanasia, i.e., a judgment that euthanasia is a bad thing. Whether the value decision is simple or complex depends upon the nature and extent of the relevant facts. If, in light of one's value criteria all the facts have positive valence, or they all have negative valence, the decision is fairly simple to make. The decision is complex and difficult when the relevant facts have conflicting valence, i.e., when some of the facts indicate the value object is good and some indicate it is not good. Then the evaluator must somehow weigh the facts and come to a decision. Most evaluative decisions which become the focus of concern in Social Studies classes are of this latter sort.

R. M. Hare has characterized the procedure used in arriving at justified value judgments as a procedure of conjecture and refutation.[3] After considering the relevant facts we make a tentative evaluation operating largely at the intuitive level.

Then we test the evaluation, attempting to show that it is defective. If the evaluation withstands all our attempts to show that it is poor, we accept it. If it fails the tests, we start again with another judgment. In testing the value judgment we assess both the relevant facts and the value principle implied by the judgment. In a complex judgment this principle may be rather complex, adjudicating the conflicting claims of the various criteria relevant to the judgment.

An example will help make this clearer. Suppose an evaluator is trying to decide whether or not the U.S. ought to withdraw from the war in Vietnam. He accepts the following facts (f) and criteria (c).

(f) 1. The war in Vietnam is primarily a civil war.

(c) 1. One country ought not enter into the civil wars of other countries.

(f) 2. U.S. withdrawal will result in a substantially reduced rate of killing.

(c) 2. It is wrong to kill or to cause a large number of killings.

(f) 3. U.S. withdrawal would reduce the level of civil strife in the U.S.

(c) 3. A stable, peaceful society is a good thing.

(f) 4. U.S. withdrawal would free U.S. resources which could be used to cope with pressing social problems in the U.S.

(c) 4. It is desirable for a society to have the resources available to handle pressing social problems.

(f) 5. U.S. withdrawal would result in a repressive, communistic society in South Vietnam.

(c) 5. Illiberal societies are undesirable and immoral.

(f) 6. The U.S. has committed itself to defending South Vietnam against takeover by the communists.

(c) 6. A nation ought to honor its commitments.

(f) 7. U.S. withdrawal would be construed as a sign of weakness and lack of resolve.

(c) 7. A nation ought not let others think it is weak or irresolute.

The evaluator comes to the conclusion that the U.S. ought to withdraw from the Vietnamese war. He comes to this decision on the basis of the first four facts listed above, and in spite of the last three. His judgment implies a complex value principle to the effect that a nation ought not be involved in a civil war to save a country from a repressive government if that involvement increases the level of killing in the war and diverts the nation's attention from pressing social problems. It is this complex value principle that must be tested and found acceptable to the evaluator.

The value principle implied by a value judgment should not be confused with value criteria. Value criteria are *brought to* the context of value decision making. A value principle *emerges* as a *product* of that decision. It is only after a value decision has been made and the reasons for it given that we know what value principle is implied by the judgment. A value judgment may call into play a number of diverse and conflicting criteria, but only one value principle is implied in any value judgment.

The value object commonly has a number of features or aspects. These are described by factual statements about the value object. Each value criterion provides the basis for evaluating *one particular feature* of the value object, giving either positive or negative valence to that feature. Thus the value criteria we bring to a complex value judgment enable us to evaluate each feature of the value object *separately*. They do not provide the basis for evaluating the value object as a whole. In contrast, the value principle implied in our judgment does apply to the value object as a whole and so provides the basis for our decision about the object. It is a complex principle which adjudicates the claims of the various diverse and conflicting criteria. It reflects the relative strength of the various criteria in the context of this evaluation.

Standards of Rational Value Judgment

It is now possible to specify in general terms the conditions which a value judgment must meet to qualify as rational or defensible.

1. The purported facts supporting the judgment must be true or well confirmed.

2. The facts must be genuinely relevant, i.e., they must actually have valence for the person making the judgment.

3. Other things being equal, the greater the range of relevant facts taken into account in making the judgment, the more adequate the judgment is likely to be.

4. The value principle implied by the judgment must be acceptable to the person making the judgment.

The first standard follows from the fact that value judgments are to a degree based on factual considerations. If someone is wrong about the facts, his judgment based on the facts may also be wrong. Suppose someone judges that capital punishment is a good thing on the grounds that it deters serious crime. If as a matter of fact capital punishment does not act as a deterrent, the evaluator has made a poor judgment. If the factual mistake were pointed out to the evaluator he would have to reconsider and perhaps change his judgment.

The second standard follows from the fact that a value judgment is based in part on certain of the evaluator's attitudes toward facts about the value object. If an evaluator misrepresents his attitudes towards the facts, especially to himself, he is liable to make a judgment he could not accept or defend were he to become aware of the misrepresentation. Thus his judgment is not as rational as it could be.

The third standard is implied by the dependence of value judgments on facts. Suppose someone were to judge that building freeways into cities is a good thing because freeways move persons and goods into and out of the city faster and with fewer chances of accidents occurring. He does not take into account the facts that building freeways increases congestion and air pollution in the cities. If these additional facts were pointed out to the evaluator he very well might change his original judgment. Again, this indicates that his original judgment was not as rational as it might have been.

The fourth standard of rationality derives from the fact that one cannot accept a value judgment and reject the value principle implied by it without involving himself in a logical contradiction.

Objectives of Value Analysis

It is now possible to begin to answer some of the questions about objectives of value analysis raised at the beginning of this chapter. These questions, you will remember, had to do with the meaning and legitimacy of four possible objectives.

1. Teaching students to rate a value object in a particular way.

2. Helping students to make the most rational judgment they can make about the value object in question.

3. Teaching students to make rational value judgments.

4. Teaching students how to operate as members of a group attempting to come to a common value judgment about some value object.

A person adopting the first objective may attempt to teach either of two sorts of value conclusions. He may attempt to teach that some *single* object is to be rated a given way, e.g., the present draft law is unfair. Alternatively, he may attempt to teach a value criterion, i.e., that some *class* of value objects is to be rated in a given way, other things being equal. Given the validity of the argument thus far, it seems unlikely that teaching the first sort of value conclusion could be upheld as a defensible, educational objective. This follows from two features of value judgments. First, it is only the process of evaluative reasoning, not the conclusion of it, that can be judged adequate or inadequate. Second, the standards of rationality specify, among other things, the way in which the evaluator is to relate his *own* attitudes and preferences, embodied in value criteria, to facts in coming to an evaluative decision. Thus the teacher may conclude that X is good using evaluative reasoning that meets all the standards of rationality. Still the student's value criteria might be such that he could never come to the conclusion that X is good as the result of rational evaluative reasoning.

The legitimacy of teaching value criteria is not easily decided. Nothing in our discussion provides convincing arguments for not teaching any value criteria. Each criterion must be scrutinized independently. There are, I think, good grounds for teaching some value criteria and no good grounds for teaching others. Arguments for and against individual criteria are beyond the scope of this yearbook. Persons interested in such arguments should consult the book by Peters listed in the bibliography at the end of this chapter.

As indicated earlier, the second and third possible objectives of value analysis are viable only if there are standards of rationality applicable to value judgments. Our inquiry into the nature of evaluative reasoning indicates that such standards can be specified. No elaborate arguments need be advanced to show that these objectives are also worth achieving. Increasing the rationality of the conduct of students has long been accepted as an important objective of education in our society.

Nothing we have discovered about evaluative reasoning indicates that the objective of teaching students how to resolve value conflicts is insupportable. Since value judgments can not be proved true or false, and since they are not of such a nature that agreement is always more important than the value conclusion agreed upon, we can teach no techniques that will ensure success in resolving value conflicts. Still there are some things we can teach which will increase the chances that students will be successful without compromising the rationality of their judgments. Rational resolution of value conflict requires that the disputants identify the source of the conflict. Students can be taught the possible sources of disagreement such that they can pinpoint where the controversy arises in any particular case. Conflict can arise over (1) the truth of some factual claim, (2) the relevance of a given fact, (3) the valence of a given fact, (4) the interpretation of a particular value criterion, or (5) the acceptability of the value principle implied in the judgment.

Returning to the Vietnamese war example cited earlier, we see that conflicting value judgments could result from disagreement over the truth of the factual claim that U.S. withdrawal would result in other nations thinking the U.S. is weak. There may be disagreement about the relevance of the fact that this would be the first time the U.S. military has been unsuccessful in a war. Some persons may have criteria relating this fact to some evaluation; others may not have such criteria. There may be disagreement over the valence of the fact that U.S. withdrawal is likely to result in a communistic regime in South Vietnam. Some persons may have criteria rating this fact positively, while others may rate it negatively. Disagreement may arise over the interpretation of the value criterion that one nation ought not be allowed to impose its will on another nation by force. Some persons may interpret "nation" in such a way as to regard South Vietnam as a nation. Others may interpret "nation" in such a way as to regard South Vietnam as part of one nation including both North and South Vietnam. Finally, a dispute may arise because some persons accept the value principle implied by the judgment that the U.S. should withdraw from the Vietnamese war while others cannot accept the principle.

Exactly what we are trying to achieve when we aim for objectives two and three is made clear by our discussion of evaluative reasoning. Achieving the second objective means getting each student to make a value judgment using a reasoning process which meets, insofar as possible, all the standards of rationality described above. The third objective entails teaching students to adhere to the standards of rationality in making future value judgments. This objective is much more ambitious than the second and undoubtedly cannot be achieved by a single value analysis. Students must be taught how to gather facts, how to determine the relevancy of facts, how to assess the accuracy of factual claims, and how to test the acceptability of the value principles implicit in their judgments. In addition they must be taught the disposition to do these things when they make important value judgments.

Some elaboration is necessary to make clear what is involved in testing the acceptability of the principle implicit in one's judgment. Several different tests of these principles are possible. One test involves making the principle explicit, imagining other situations in which it would apply, and deciding if one can accept its application in these other situations. An example should make this clearer. Teacher Novice has tentatively decided that Frank, a boy with a winning personality, is a good student. The facts he gives as reasons for his decision are that Frank always does his assignments neatly and on time, and averages 55 percent on his examinations. In order to test his implied value principle, Mr. Novice explicitly formulates it as follows: any student who does his assignments neatly and on time and averages at least 55 percent on his examinations is a good student. He then tests it by seeing if he can accept it when it is applied to other students. John, a quiet, colorless boy, meets all the conditions specified in the value principle, but Mr. Novice just cannot accept the judgment that he is a good student. This means the principle is unacceptable to Mr. Novice and he must reconsider his judgment.

A second way of determining the acceptability of a value principle is by trying to find reasons, i.e., relevant facts and more general value principles, which justify it. If one can construct such a justification he has good grounds for accepting the principle. Consider this example. The unrestricted use of D.D.T. to control pests is judged as inadvisable on the grounds that it needlessly endangers the health of people and animals. The principle implied here is that it is inadvisable to act in such a way as to endanger the health of persons and animals needlessly. The evaluator then determines the acceptability of this principle by finding out if there are relevant facts and more general principles to support it. He judges that it is acceptable because he accepts the following fact and general principle which support it.

FACT: *Anything which endangers the health of animals and persons increases the possibility that they will suffer.*

MORE GENERAL
VALUE PRINCIPLE: *It is inadvisable to increase needlessly the possibility that human beings and animals will suffer.*

These first two tests can be used to determine the acceptability of the principle implied in virtually any sort of value judgment. The two tests discussed below are applicable only to *moral* judgments about actions or practices. The third means of testing the value principle does not entail making the principle explicit. It is accomplished by the evaluator's exchanging roles with other persons affected by the judgment. If he can still accept the judgment when taking these other roles he can accept the principle implied by the judgment.[4] In the case of the previous example concerning U.S. withdrawal from the war in Vietnam, the evaluator might take the role of a South Vietnamese. If he were a South Vietnamese, could he still agree that the U.S. ought to withdraw from the war? If he cannot agree, then he cannot accept the principle implied in the judgment and so must reconsider his evaluation. If he can still accept the judgment he may further test the principle by adopting the role of some other interested party. The most crucial test is provided by exchanging roles with the person likely to be most adversely affected by the judgment.

The fourth test for determining the acceptability of a value principle is similar to the third in that it does not involve making the principle explicit. In this test the evaluator asks "What would be the consequences if everyone (in this sort of circumstance) were to act in the way the value judgment recommends?" If the consequences of everyone's acting in this way are unacceptable, then the principle implied in the judgment is unacceptable.[5] Suppose someone tentatively decides it is all right for him to burn his trash in the back yard. The circumstances are that he wants to use the money he would have to pay a trash collector for something else. By itself his trash burning would not make the air detrimental to plant or animal life. To test the principle implied in his judgment he asks, "What would happen if everyone in this circumstance were to burn trash in his back yard?" He decides that the consequences of this would be air pollution detrimental to animal and plant life. Since this consequence is unacceptable to him, the principle implied in his judgment is unacceptable.

Some Further Considerations

In the first section of this chapter we noted that value judgments can be made from a number of different points of view, e.g., aesthetic, moral, prudential points of view. We also noted that one can make an overall judgment of the advisability, desirability, or goodness of a value object. Different sets of facts are relevant to judgments from different points of view. For example, a judgment of the efficiency of the anti-poverty program would take into account somewhat different facts than those taken into account in judging the morality of the program.

Judgments from different points of view are often interrelated. That is to say, coming to a decision about a value object from one point of view often helps us come to a decision about the value object from a second point of view. Suppose someone is trying to judge whether a public health program is a good thing from the moral point of view. In the course of his deliberation he decides that the program is inefficient. This judgment may be an important factor in his moral judgment. He may decide the program is immoral because its inefficiency allows suffering that could be avoided. Judging a value object from different points of view may also be helpful in coming to a decision about the overall worth of the value object. For example, if we are trying to judge the worth of a certain car, it is helpful to decide whether or not it is safe, economical, beautiful, and dependable. Value judgments which are component parts of another value decision we call "subsidiary judgments." In the example above value judgments about the safety, beauty, and economy of the car are subsidiary to the judgment of the overall worth of the car. Each of these subsidiary judgments sums up a certain range of facts about the value object from a given value point of view. When one is faced with a large, complex body of facts relevant to his judgment he may choose to reduce the complexity by making a number of subsidiary judgments, each from a different point of view. He must then weigh the various subsidiary judgments and make his primary, overall value decision.

Judgments from the moral point of view are of particular interest because in a sense they take precedence over judgments from all other points of view. A judgment that the value object is *the* morally right thing to do or that it is morally bad overrides all other judgments of the value object. Only when the value object is neither morally required nor morally prohibited do judgments from other points of view determine the overall worth of the value object. Forcible sterilization may be judged an effective way to control population. However, if we also judge the practice to be immoral, then our overall judgment must be that it is not a good practice. If we judge smoking to be neither morally required nor morally wrong, our judgment of its worth will be decided by considerations relevant to other points of view, e.g., health. Moral judgments are distinguished from other sorts of value judgments by the fact that they are based on equal and impartial consideration of the interests of everyone concerned.

Up to this point we have written as though value objects are always judged in isolation from other things. Actually many value judgments are comparative. We try to decide if the value object is better or worse than something else or if it is the best of some set of alternatives. For example, we may try to decide if socialized medicine is better than private prepaid medical insurance or if urban renewal is the best way to improve housing in slum areas. When value judgments are comparative, relevant facts are those which allow us to compare the value object with its alternatives. Value criteria and the value principles implied by the judgment are also stated in comparative terms.

Current fashion in educational theorizing encourages us to conceptualize educational objectives as being either cognitive behaviors or affective behaviors, or a set of behaviors both cognitive and affective. Testing student achievement is then viewed as a process of observing to see if students exhibit the appropriate behaviors in appropriate circumstances.

It is instructive to consider the objective of helping students make rational judgments about the value object in question from this point of view. Is our objective to produce a cognitive outcome in the student or an affective outcome? Are we perhaps attempting to produce some outcomes of each type? These questions are difficult to answer. Arriving at a rational value judgment engages both the cognitive and affective aspects of a person's makeup. It involves the evaluator's cognitive structure because it requires knowledge of facts and the ability to test them. It involves the affective makeup of the evaluator because it is dependent on commitment to value criteria and principles, both of which embody feelings, attitudes, and preferences. When a person holds a rational evaluative conclusion there are some things he knows and some things he feels. The difficulty is that we cannot specify that the student must know specific things A, B and C and that he must have feeling D. What he must know is dependent to a degree on what he feels. Conversely, what he feels is determined by what he knows. We come back to the point emphasized earlier: the outcome sought is that students will have acted according to certain standards in making their decisions. It is difficult to see how this outcome could be described in terms of the cognitive-affective behaviors dichotomy. Assessment of student achievement with respect to this objective must be based primarily on performance during value analysis, not on behaviors exhibited after it.

Summary

The primary focus of this chapter has been to answer the question, "What exactly are the legitimate objectives of value analysis in the classroom?" We have attempted to answer this question by examining the logic of value judgment and justification. In so doing we have argued the following points.

1. It is possible to describe our use of value language and the rules governing our reasoning about matters of value without thereby making any value judgments.

2. Value judgments are neither judgments of fact nor mere expressions of attitude.

3. Standards of rational value judgment can be specified but they apply to the process of value decision making not to the product of such a decision. These standards include:

   a. The purported facts supporting the judgment must be true or well confirmed.

   b. The facts must be genuinely relevant, i.e., they must actually have valence for the person making the judgment.

   c. Other things being equal, the greater the range of relevant facts taken into account in making the judgment, the more adequate the judgment is likely to be.

   d. The value principle implied by the judgment must be acceptable to the person making the judgment.

4. Since standards of rational value judgment can be specified the following objectives of value analysis in the classroom are defensible.

   a. Helping students make the most rational, defensible value judgments they can make.

   b. Helping students acquire the capabilities necessary to make rational value decisions and the disposition to do so.

5. There are no logical grounds for deciding that value criteria ought never to be taught nor for deciding that resolution of conflict about value matters is an illegitimate objective of value analysis.

NOTES

[1] For an extensive discussion of points of view see Georg Henrik von Wright, *The Varieties of Goodness* (London: Routledge & Kegan Paul, 1963).

[2] Paul W. Taylor, *Normative Discourse* (Englewood Cliffs, N.J.: Prentice-Hall, Inc., 1961), pp. 115-117.

[3] R. M. Hare, *Freedom and Reason* (New York: Oxford University Press, 1965), pp. 87-92.

[4] This principle is suggested and discussed at length in *ibid.*, pp. 90-95.

[5] This principle is expounded in Marcus Singer, *Generalization in Ethics* (London: Eyre & Spottiswoode, 1963), pp. 61-96.

SELECTED READINGS
IN THE LOGIC OF VALUE JUDGMENT

Baier, Kurt. *The Moral Point of View*. Ithaca, New York: Cornell University Press, 1958.

Frankena, William. *Ethics*. Englewood Cliffs, N.J.: Prentice-Hall, Inc., 1963.

Hare, R. M. *Freedom and Reason*. New York: Oxford University Press, 1963.

Peters, Richard S. *Ethics and Education*. London: George Allen & Unwin Ltd., 1966.

Singer, Marcus G. *Generalization in Ethics*. London: Eyre & Spottiswoode, 1963.

Taylor, Paul W. *Normative Discourse*. Englewood Cliffs, N.J.: Prentice-Hall, Inc., 1961.

von Wright, Georg H. *The Varieties of Goodness*. London: Routledge & Kegan Paul, 1963.

Wilson, John. *Reason and Morals*. Cambridge University Press, 1961.

Wilson, John, Norman Williams, and Barry Sugarman. *Introduction to Moral Education*. Baltimore: Penguin Books, 1967.

2

Teaching Strategies for Value Analysis

JERROLD R. COOMBS AND MILTON MEUX

☐ In the first chapter of this book we argued that there are at least three defensible objectives of analysis and deliberation about controversial value issues in Social Studies classes. These objectives include: (1) helping students make the most rational decisions they can make about the value issue under consideration, (2) helping students develop the capabilities and dispositions required for making rational value decisions, and (3) teaching students how to resolve value conflict between themselves and other members of a group. The purpose of the present chapter is to discuss ways in which teachers might conduct value analyses to secure these objectives.

In any evaluative decision-making process the following six tasks must be carried out.

1. Identifying and clarifying the value question

2. Assembling (gathering and organizing) purported facts

3. Assessing the truth of purported facts

4. Clarifying the relevance of facts

5. Arriving at a tentative value decision

6. Testing the value principle implied in the decision

To help students make the most rational decisions they can make about the value issue at hand the teacher must ensure that these tasks are performed in such a way as to fulfill the standards of rational value judgment. Helping students develop the capabilities and dispositions required for making rational value decisions entails teaching students to perform these six tasks adequately on their own. Consequently, our discussion of strategies teachers can use to attain these two objectives will center around the intellectual operations involved in performing each of these six tasks and the ways in which the teacher might manage their performance.

There are a number of things we think it useful to say about conducting a value analysis so as to ensure that these six tasks are adequately performed. Unfortunately, there is little we feel entitled to say about the best way to conduct a value analysis so as to help students learn to perform these six tasks adequately on their own. The research necessary to provide sound prescriptions about this matter has not yet been conducted. What little we do have to say must be considered as tentative hypotheses. As indicated in the second part of this chapter, development of the capability for rational evaluation is a complex and lengthy process, closely associated with a person's ego development. It seems unlikely, then, that very much can be accomplished through a *single* value analysis. Further, there are many learning activities outside the context of value analysis which can be used to help develop students' capabilities for rational evaluation. Thus this objective must be viewed as a long-range goal to be achieved in part by involving students in many value analyses.

Our general hypotheses concerning the best means of fostering a student's capability for rational evaluation through value analyses are as follows:

1. The teacher should *actively* engage the student in the operations required to carry out each of the six tasks described above. As the student's familiarity with these operations increases, he should be given increased responsibility for initiating them and carrying them out on his own.

2. The teacher should point out what task is to be accomplished by each of the operations in which he engages students.

3. The teacher should point out the importance of each of these tasks in terms of meeting the standards of rational evaluation.

In the ensuing discussion of strategies we shall attempt to spell out the implications of these hypotheses in more specific terms.

I. Identifying and Clarifying the Value Question

The value question, i.e., the question which gives rise to discussion or deliberation about a value issue, is often vague or ambiguous. Such a question may be unclear in several different ways. The question may not make clear the point of view from which the value object is to be judged. Consider this value question. "Should students take over university buildings to call attention to their grievances?" It is not clear from the question whether we are being asked to judge the action of taking over university buildings from the point of view of effectiveness or from the moral point of view.

The value question may be unclear also because it does not clearly specify the value object we are being asked to judge. This may result from an elliptical or cryptic statement of the question or from ambiguity or vagueness of the term used to refer to the value object. The question "Is it all right to use drugs?" does not clearly specify the value object we are being asked to judge. We don't know whether it means all drugs, including penicillin, sulfa, etc., or whether it means only hallucinogenic drugs. We don't know whether it means using drugs for any purpose including medicinal and therapeutic purposes or only for the purpose of obtaining thrills. We don't know whether it means using alcohol and tobacco or only such drugs as heroin and L.S.D. The vagueness of this question stems both from the fact that it is elliptically stated and from the fact that the word "drug" is vague. Consider another value question: "Is socialized medicine a good thing?" On first glance this question appears to be clear enough. Closer consideration reveals that the phrase "socialized medicine" is vague. Does the medicare plan constitute socialized medicine? Does socialized medicine mean doctors will be paid a salary by the government? Different persons may very well answer these questions differently. They may not know precisely what meaning to give to the phrase "socialized medicine."

When the value question is unclear, discussion or deliberation about value issues tends to be confused, perplexing, and frustrating. Not knowing exactly what they are trying to evaluate or the point of view from which they are being asked to make the evaluation, students become confused as to what facts are relevant to the evaluation and how they are relevant. Our experience indicates that this confusion quickly leads to frustration. Students come to feel that the value question is just too complex and difficult for them to deal with.

It is fairly easy to get clarity concerning the point of view from which the evaluation is to be made. If the teacher has raised the value question, he can avoid confusion by indicating clearly the point of view from which the evaluation is to be made and the points of view which are not relevant. Suppose the teacher asks the question "Should students take over university buildings to call attention to their grievances?" He might avoid confusion by indicating that he does not want students to judge whether or not this action is effective, but whether it is a morally acceptable action. If the value question has been raised by a student the teacher may seek clarification by indicating the various points of view and asking the student which of them is to be taken in making the evaluation.

If the value question is unclear because the term used to refer to the value object is vague or ambiguous, clarity may be provided in several ways. One means of providing clarity is that of defining the term. For example, the value question "Is socialized medicine a good thing?" may be clarified by defining the term "socialized medicine." This means of providing clarity is limited, however, by the fact that it is often very difficult to provide satisfactory definitions of such terms.

The second means of clarifying the meaning of the term used to refer to the value object is that of providing examples of things to which the term refers and examples of things to which the term does not refer. It is usually easier to provide examples of this sort than it is to define the term. In addition, the examples are likely to be more meaningful and better understood by students than is a more abstract definition. If one were to clarify the term "socialized medicine" in this way he might describe the national health scheme in England and identify it as a case of socialized medicine. He might identify the Federal-Provincial health insurance plan in Canada as a case of socialized medicine. He might describe the Medicare plan and cite it as not being an example of socialized medicine. Pointing out differences between examples of things to which the term refers and examples of things to which it does not refer also helps provide clarity, as does giving the reasons why the term does or does not apply to each of the examples.

In considering how the teacher should manage the clarification of the value question we must keep in mind that the teacher has a dual purpose here: that of clarifying the value question so that students can make a rational evaluation in response to it, and that of teaching students how to clarify value questions. Let us consider first how the teacher might achieve the first of these purposes. Value questions may be introduced into the classroom in several different ways. If the teacher raises the value question it is up to him to ask the question as clearly as possible, to clearly indicate the point of view from which the evaluation is to be made, to provide definitions of any terms which may be vague or ambiguous, to describe cases which are examples of the value object and cases which are not examples of the value object, to point out the differences between these two sorts of cases and to give reasons why each case is or is not an example of the value object. For example, a teacher might introduce and clarify a value question as follows:

There is a lot of talk about drugs these days and the use of drugs seems to be greatly increasing. This has led many people to question laws regulating the use of drugs. I would like you to consider whether or not it is morally right to pass laws prohibiting adults from taking drugs for purposes other than the treatment of physical or mental illness. By "drugs" I mean substances which alter a person's emotions, make him feel "high" or give him hallucinations by changing his body chemistry and which are also addictive, that is, the person's body comes to need them. Drugs would include such things as opium, heroin and amphetamines because these substances change a person's feelings by changing the chemical makeup of his body and they are addictive. Alcohol would not count as a drug since it is not addictive. Nor is tobacco a drug in the sense we are using the term here because it doesn't significantly change a person's emotions or give him hallucinations.

Notice that in this case the teacher identifies the point of view from which the value judgment is to be made (the moral point of view). He gives a definition of "drug," the term used to refer to the value object. He identifies examples of things which are drugs (opium, heroin, amphetamines) and things which are not drugs (tobacco, alcohol). Finally he gives reasons for regarding these substances as being examples of drugs or as not being examples of drugs.

If the value question is raised by the student the teacher may ask the student for definitions, examples, etc. Or the teacher may propose definitions and examples and ask the student if they are true to what he had in mind when he raised the value question. Suppose a student were to raise the question "Is it bad to take drugs?" The teacher might ask the following sorts of questions:

Are you asking if it is morally wrong to take drugs or do you want to know if it is bad for one's health?

Can you tell us what you mean by "taking drugs"?

Will you define the term "drug" for us?

How about giving us some examples of things you consider to be drugs?

You said marijuana is a drug. Why do you consider it to be a drug?

Would you consider alcohol to be a drug?

Why doesn't alcohol count as a drug?

Does a substance have to be addictive before it counts as a drug in your sense of the term?

In your use of the phrase "taking drugs," does it refer to taking drugs to treat physical and mental illness or does it only refer to taking drugs for non-medicinal purposes?

Many of the value questions raised in Social Studies classes will be questions currently under discussion and debate in society at large. In such cases the point of clarifying the value question is to get clear about that value issue with which our society is struggling. This means that neither the teacher nor any particular student is a special authority on what question is really being asked. Consequently, neither the students nor the teacher can be permitted to stipulate or legislate meanings for terms used to formulate the value question. Both must get clear about the meanings these terms ordinarily have by carefully considering features of cases to which the terms *ordinarily* apply and contrasting these with cases to which the terms do not apply.[1] The success of this clarifying procedure is dependent in large measure on the proposed cases being carefully and completely described.

It would appear to be better to clarify value questions of this sort through class discussion rather than through consultation between the teacher and individual students. Discussions should lead to a greater variety of cases being proposed for consideration. It should lead as well to more accurate judgments as to whether or not a term (as it is ordinarily used) applies to a particular case, since more persons will participate in making the judgments.

What we have said so far should throw some light on how the teacher can promote clarification of the value question. But how is the teacher to manage this clarification in such a way as to help students learn how to clarify value questions on their own? The following suggestions stem from our general hypotheses stated earlier. The teacher should:

1. call attention to the need for clarification of the value question.

2. explicitly identify as clarifying operations those activities he initiates to obtain clarification of the value question.

3. involve students actively in clarifying operations and increasingly require students to assume the burden of initiating clarifying operations.

Consider an example in which the class is discussing whether or not it is bad to take drugs. The teacher may call attention to the need for clarification by a remark such as the following:

I think we'd better get clear what we mean by "taking drugs." We can't really arrive at a reasonable answer to a value question until we are fairly clear about what it is asking.

The teacher may explicitly identify things that can be done to clarify a value question by remarks such as these:

Let's consider some examples of things we would consider to be drugs and examples of similar things that we don't regard as drugs. This should help us to become clear about what we are evaluating.

We can get clearer about what we mean by "drug taking" if we consider the differences between cases we consider to be drug taking and cases we don't want to call drug taking.

The value question you are asking would be much clearer to us if you would define what you mean by "drug."

Students can be made to assume the burden of initiating clarifying operations by the following sorts of requests or demands.

I'm not sure what that question is asking. How can we get clear about it?

Can you help us pin down just what we are supposed to be evaluating?

It is not clear when is the best time for the teacher to initiate operations to clarify the value question. On strictly logical grounds it would seem best to strive for clarity right at the beginning of the discussion or deliberation. One cannot gather relevant facts unless he knows what he is judging. However, a good argument can be made for occasionally postponing clarification until confusion develops about what facts are relevant and how they are relevant. At this point students will feel the need for clarification. If clarifying operations are always carried out at the beginning of the evaluation, students may come to regard them as pointless intellectual exercises because they have never felt the need for them.

II. Assembling Facts

As was pointed out in Chapter 1, every value judgment is based on some factual considerations. This means that an important part of any value analysis teaching strategy is managing the assembling of facts relevant to making the value judgment. To do this job successfully the teacher must ensure that:

1. value assertions are not mistakenly assembled as part of the body of relevant facts.
2. a fairly wide range of facts relevant to judging the value object in question is assembled.
3. fact gathering is carried out in such a way as not to overwhelm students with the complexity of factual material.

DISTINGUISHING FACTUAL FROM EVALUATIVE ASSERTIONS

It is not unusual for a person who is assembling facts about a value object to make the mistake of including in his list of facts some evaluative assertion. For example, a person attempting to decide whether or not a car is good may cite as facts that it is dependable, economical, or safe. Actually these are all evaluative assertions. To be sure, there is nothing wrong with making such subsidiary judgments in the course of coming to some more inclusive value decision. However, if the value assertions of others are mistakenly regarded as factual a student may unknowingly accept an assertion based on a value criterion he does not accept. This could seriously distort his value decision.

The teacher could ensure that this does not happen by personally assembling all the facts students are likely to find relevant. But this is not likely to teach students how to avoid this mistake when they are assembling facts on their own. It would seem to be more useful to proceed by providing students with cues for distinguishing factual from evaluative assertions,[2] cautioning them to avoid confusing the two types of claims when gathering facts, setting them to gathering facts and then correcting them when they mistakenly include an evaluative claim in their assembled facts, and explaining to them why the statement is evaluative rather than factual. The teacher should also point out the importance of not mistaking value assertions for factual ones.

ASSEMBLING A FAIRLY WIDE RANGE OF FACTS

The most important facts to gather in coming to a value decision are those which indicate how the value object affects the significant interests and concerns of *people*. These interests and concerns are of several different kinds. Some of the more significant kinds of concerns include concern for economic welfare, concern for health, concern for recreation, concern for aesthetic enjoyment, and concern for freedom. It often happens that persons make poor value judgments because they neglect to assemble facts related to one of these important areas of concern. The assembly of a wide range of facts can be promoted by collecting facts related to as many of these concerns as possible. Another way of ensuring the assembly of a wide range of facts is that of seeking expert testimony from a range of persons having diverse backgrounds and points of view.

The teacher can ensure that a wide range of facts is assembled by collecting the facts himself. He may want to do this in some cases. For example, he may want to save time so that he can spend more time on some other aspect of the value decision-making process. A teacher would be unwise to restrict himself to this mode of operation because it does little to teach students how to make sure that they collect a wide range of facts when they are making evaluations on their own. The following suggestions are offered as reasonable hypotheses concerning the most useful way of managing the assembling of a wide range of facts.

1. When instructing students to gather facts, call attention to the importance of assembling a fairly wide range of facts.
2. Provide students with a list of basic human concerns or help them draw up such a list. Instruct them to gather facts about the value object related to as many of these concerns as possible.
3. Encourage and aid students to identify a variety of sources of information about the value object. Instruct them to gather facts about the value object from as many of these sources as possible.

Teaching students the library and research skills needed for gathering facts is the focus of a considerable amount of schooling. We have nothing new to add to the large body of literature describing these skills and the best way of teaching them. Suffice it to point out that assembling facts to make a value decision provides a very good opportunity for the practice of these skills.

HANDLING COMPLEXITY

The facts relative to making a decision about a controversial value question are in most cases both numerous and diverse. They are diverse in that they relate to different domains of human experience, and they are of differing degrees of abstractness and generality. Further, general facts vary in the amount of evidence that supports them. This large body of diverse facts in many cases overwhelms the student. He does not know how to cope with them. Consequently he may throw up his hands in frustration claiming that no one can make sense of this diffuse mass of facts and so come to a reasonable decision.

Much more empirical research is needed before we can say with confidence how the problem of complexity may be solved. The best we can do here is to offer the following suggestions which in our experience appear to be beneficial.

1. Have the student organize facts as they are collected by different concerns. Thus, if we are assembling facts to determine the desirability of building an airport on the edge of the Everglades we may divide facts into groups according to whether they indicate (a) the economic effects of building the airport, (b) the effects of the airport on recreational concerns, (c) the effects of the airport on the aesthetic environment, (d) the effects of the airport on the health and safety of persons. This sort of grouping of facts helps reduce confusion by making facts distinguishable yet relating them to other facts.

2. Have the student distinguish facts on the basis of whether they support a positive or a negative rating. It is useful to list facts as they are collected in parallel columns under the headings "positive" and "negative." Such listings might be made for each concern. In addition to providing a further way of differentiating and relating facts this procedure assembles facts in such a way as to indicate their relevance to the value decision to be made.

3. Have the student subsume specific facts under more general facts for which they provide evidence. Suppose one is attempting to decide whether or not the Selective Service System is fair. He may find it claimed that the Selective Service System brings into the army a higher proportion of Negroes than Whites. He may read in another place that a town having only 20 percent Negroes had more Negroes than Whites drafted in a given year. This latter claim serves as evidence for the first, more general, claim. Consequently, it is useful to group it under the more general claim.

4. Have the student be on the alert for the same facts expressed in different terms. These should be amalgamated when one is assembling facts.

5. Have the student periodically suspend fact gathering to rank the already assembled facts with respect to how important they appear to be to the value decision to be made. Facts having very low significance, i.e., those unlikely to make any difference to the decision, may be deleted.

6. When possible, have the student sum up the facts related

to a given concern by arriving at a judgment of the worth of the value object from the point of view of that concern. These judgments are subsidiary to the primary value decision to be made. Again, suppose one is assembling facts to determine the desirability of building an airport on the edge of the Everglades. We may sum up facts related to the concern for recreation by the subsidiary judgment that the airport would be very undesirable from the recreational point of view. It helps to include in these subsidiary judgments some indication of the strength of the rating. One should, for example, indicate whether something is just slightly detrimental, fairly detrimental, or highly detrimental from a given point of view. This gives us a cue as to how much weight the subsidiary rating should be given in the primary value decision.

It is not always possible to reduce complexity by summing up facts in a subsidiary rating. In some cases the primary rating itself is to be made from only one point of view.

7. When possible, allow students to work at their own pace in assembling facts. There are good grounds for believing that students differ with respect to the rate at which they can assimilate facts and grasp their relevance for making a given value decision. If facts are presented to a student too rapidly, there is a danger that he may become frustrated or that he will have a distorted perception of the facts.

8. Explain to students why it is important to reduce complexity.

9. Point out to students that the function of each of the procedures described in 1-7 above is to help them organize and make sense of complex bodies of facts.

THE FACT-ASSEMBLY CHART

Several of these suggestions for handling complexity — especially points 1, 2, 3, and 6 — may be combined into a chart which further systematizes the student's assembly of facts. This further systematization should help the student see the issue more "as a whole."

The optimum use of the chart probably takes place after the student has already read a considerable amount of material, and thus has a sense of what his most relevant concerns are in the issue, what some of the main positive and negative facts are, and which facts are serving as evidence for the other facts.

Although the student will probably work with a single sheet of paper, he may wish to try other arrangements before he finalizes the chart. For example, he may write each fact on a separate slip of paper and try different organizations of the facts on a bulletin board or opaque projector. In our experience, it has been fruitful to allow the students some freedom in developing their own formats, and in some cases their developments have turned out to be more useful than our own.

The form of the chart we are suggesting is shown in Figure 1.

Figure 1. **Chart for Systematizing Assembly of Facts**

| | | Negative | | Positive | | Subsidiary |
		General	Specific	General	Specific	Value Judgments
	A					
Student's	B					
Basic						
Concerns	C					
	D					

The student's own basic concerns are at the left of the chart; he may have only one or two concerns or he may have six or seven. The positive and negative headings are at the top of the chart in the main left section. Within the positive section the general facts and the specific facts serving as evidence are separated. The negative section is also subdivided into the general and specific facts. Finally, the main right section of the chart contains the subsidiary value judgments, one for each of the student's basic concerns.

An example of the use of this chart is shown in Figure 2. The value object or issue is "Use of DDT." Because of space limitations only a few of the person's purported facts are included for each concern.

| | Value Object: Use of DDT | | | | | |
| Basic Concerns | POSITIVE | | NEGATIVE | | Subsidiary Value Judgments |
	General	Specific	General	Specific	
Ecology			DDT gets concentrated in the food chain so that animals & people at the end of the food chain get concent. DDT DDT destroys natural controls and balances in pests	Lake Michigan study 0.0085 ppm in sediment 0.41 ppm in tiny invertebrates 3-8 ppm in flesh of fish eating invertebrates 3,177 ppm in fatty tissue of gulls feeding on fish Trillionths in rain and surface water 5-20 ppm in fatty tissues of people	Highly detrimental
Economic	DDT has a large market DDT costs less than alternative methods of control		DDT costs more than formerly	See decreasing power to kill insects	Much less useful and effective
Practical	DDT is persistent DDT kills a broad range of insects DDT's alternatives cost more and require more ingenuity to find	Resists breakdown by water, microbes, and sunlight Flies, mosquitoes, bollworm Harder marketing methods More specialized controls New research needed	DDT is decreasing in power to kill insects DDT has available alternatives	Use on cotton tripled from 1965 to 1967 In Texas, dose needed to kill bollworm increased many 1000-fold 1960-65 Plants resistant to insects Introducing natural enemies	Risky Self-defeating
Health	DDT combats malaria	Experience in Panama and other parts of world	DDT may affect sex-hormone metabolism	Birds & mammals have similar sex hormones and regulators High DDT levels in autopsies of humans	Probably dangerous

Figure 2. Example of Fact-Assembly Chart, with the Value Object "Use of DDT"

III. Assessing Factual Assertions

In the fact-assembling phase of a value analysis a number of purportedly factual statements will have been collected. If students are to make responsible value decisions, these decisions must be based on factual assertions which are true or well-supported by evidence. This means the teacher must ensure that students have good grounds for the factual claims they accept.

Facts relevant to a value decision may be of three kinds: (1) particular facts, (2) general facts, (3) conditional facts. A particular factual assertion describes a *single* event or state of affairs. The following statements assert particular facts.

The U.S. has more than 300,000 troops in Viet Nam.

In 1969 the U.S. Congress appropriated more money to fight the war in Viet Nam than it did to fight poverty and pollution in the U.S.

More than 30,000 U.S. military personnel have been killed in Viet Nam since 1965.

The statements below express general facts, i.e., empirical generalizations.

DDT can kill fish and birds.

Most of our milk contains DDT.

Automobile exhaust emits unburned hydrocarbons.

Conditional facts are expressed in the statements below.

If the U.S. pulls its troops out of South Viet Nam, it will fall to the Communists.

If the U.S. withdraws from Viet Nam, other nations will no longer believe what U.S. spokesmen say.

If the U.S. invades North Viet Nam, China will enter the war against the U.S.

Particular factual assertions may be verified by observing the event or state of affairs the assertion describes. For example the truth of the claim that the U.S. has more than

300,000 troops in Viet Nam could be determined by counting the U.S. soldiers in Viet Nam. General factual assertions are verified or falsified by finding particular facts which support or refute them. We find out whether or not it is true that DDT kills birds and animals by observing those that have eaten DDT and seeing if they die. Conditional factual assertions ("if-then" assertions) are verified by finding out whether or not anything similar to the "then" part of the assertion has in the past followed the occurrence of things similar to what is described in the "if" part of the assertion. Suppose we wanted to determine the truth of the assertion that if the U.S. withdraws from Viet Nam, other nations will no longer believe what U.S. spokesmen say. We would look to see what were the results in past cases in which a nation reversed its stated policy of fighting in defense of a particular government.

In most cases neither the teacher nor the students are able to verify the assembled factual assertions in this firsthand manner. Rather they must rely on official records, eyewitness accounts, and the testimony of experts. In other words, they must assess factual assertions by assessing the source of the assertion. This type of assessment includes finding out whether or not the person who has made the factual assertion is in a position to know the facts, i.e., has access to the facts; has the acumen, experience, and training to assess the situation accurately; has a reputation for veracity and reliability; has nothing to gain by deceiving others about the facts in question; and is supported in his opinion by other experts.

In some cases the assessment of a factual claim presents special problems because the claim is vague or ambiguous. Students must be taught how to cope with such problems. Suppose a student is attempting to decide whether or not abortion is wrong. He accepts a value criterion to the effect that it is wrong to deliberately kill another person and is attempting to determine the truth of the factual claim that abortion involves the deliberate killing of a person. At first glance this factual claim seems obviously true. On reflection we begin to have some doubts. The term "person" is vague. It could mean any member of the human species at any stage of development after conception; or it could mean a member of the human species having all the attributes that confer person-hood, namely consciousness, hopes, fears, expectations, emo-tions, etc. Interpretations falling somewhere between these two extremes are also possible. Before the evaluator can assess the factual claim, he must resolve this vagueness. He must decide exactly what "person" means in this context. This de-cision is far from arbitrary. "Person" must mean the same thing in the factual claim as it means in the value criterion, otherwise the purported fact will not be relevant to the value judgment under consideration. To decide the precise nature of the factual claim, then, the evaluator must determine what "person" means in the value criterion to which he is committed.

How can the teacher manage the assessment of facts so as to ensure that students make their value decisions on the basis of accurate facts and at the same time help students learn to assess facts on their own? Our tentative suggestions are that the teacher call attention to the importance of assessing the purported facts, and actively engage the students in fact-assessing activities. The teacher may elect to engage students in fact assessment ,by questioning them about the factual assertions they have collected. He may, for example, ask such questions as :

How do you know this is true?

What evidence is there to indicate that this is true?

Who said this is the case?

Why should we believe what this person says?

Do other authorities agree with what he says?

If the teacher adopts this questioning technique it is probably useful for him to call attention to the function of these ques-tions in promoting assessment of the facts. He must also make it clear that these questions are meant only to put purported facts to the test and do not imply any personal criticism of the student who has collected the presumed facts.

If the teacher elects not to promote assessment by asking questions of students, he may provide each student with a set of questions that he can ask himself or that he can ask other students to get their views on the truth of the factual assertions. Any group discussions directed toward assessing factual assertions should be carefully monitored by the teacher to rule out irrelevant or illegitimate questions, e.g., questions about the acceptability of value criteria and personal attacks on the other students.

IV. Clarifying the Relevance of Facts

It was pointed out in the first chapter of this yearbook that facts are relevant to a given value decision when they are facts about the value object being judged, and when the evaluator has criteria giving them positive or negative valence from the point of view of the value judgment being made. Rarely does anyone make the mistake of taking into consideration facts which are not facts about the value object being judged unless he is confused about the value object. More common is the mistake of taking into consideration facts which do not have valence from the point of view of the judgment being made. For example, suppose someone were attempting to decide whether or not a judge is morally fit to sit on the Supreme Court. He may take into consideration the fact that a number of trials over which the judge presided were reversed for procedural mistakes. While this fact may have valence in deciding the *overall* competence of the judge the evaluator may be confused in thinking it relevant to a decision about the judge's competence from a *moral* point of view.

A person may also make the mistake of giving weight to a fact that really has no valence for him at all. This happens when the evaluator for some reason deceives himself about the criteria he holds, or unquestioningly accepts as relevant, facts which his friends and acquaintances regard as relevant. Consider a case in which someone is trying to decide whether or not poor people ought to be supported by public funds through relief and welfare programs. He may regard as having negative valence the fact that people would be getting money without working for it. He has heard many people cite this as a reason for not having relief programs, but does he himself have any strong conviction that people should get only the benefits they earn? He may not have such a conviction. He may merely have given weight to the fact because among his friends it is the accepted thing to do.

An evaluator may determine the relevance of a given fact by formulating as clearly as possible the criterion he believes gives valence to the fact, then carefully considering: (1) whether or not the criterion represents a judgment from the same point of view as that from which the value decision is to be made, (2) whether this criterion represents what *he* *really* believes, and (3) whether he has any good reasons for believing it. If the evaluator decides he does not really believe what the criterion asserts, the fact in question is not relevant. In the first example above the evaluator may formulate his criterion as follows:

> Judges who make a large number of procedural mistakes in trials are not fit to be Supreme Court justices.

Since his value decision is to be made from the moral point of view he must consider whether or not the phrase "not fit" in this case means "morally not fit." If it does not have this meaning, the fact in question is not relevant to his value decision. To determine the relevance of the fact in the second example above, the evaluator may formulate this criterion: "People should not get benefits they have not earned." He then must carefully consider whether or not he really believes this, and whether he has good reasons for believing it. If he finds that he does not believe it, the fact in question is not relevant.

Giving weight to an irrelevant fact decreases the rationality of one's value decision. Consequently, to ensure that students make the most rational judgment they can make about the value question under consideration the teacher must encourage and aid students in checking the relevancy of the more significant facts they consider. The first step in helping a student check the relevancy of a fact is that of helping him to formulate the criterion which gives valence to the fact. There are several ways in which the teacher can do this. Suppose that in evaluating the moral rightness of "relief" a student cites the fact that relief gives money to people who haven't earned it as a reason for regarding relief as wrong. The teacher may ask the following sorts of questions:

You say relief gives money to people who haven't earned it. What does this have to do with relief being right or wrong?

You say that one of the facts that leads you to regard relief as bad is that it gives money to people who haven't earned it. Would you say, then, that people ought not to get benefits they haven't earned?

When the criterion has been formulated the teacher must get the student to consider whether or not he believes the criterion and has reasons for believing it. He might ask questions such as the following:

Consider carefully whether you really believe that it is wrong for people to get things they haven't earned. Make sure this isn't something you say you believe just because you think other people expect you to believe it.

Do you have good reasons for this belief or have you just accepted it because you have heard lots of people say it?

In asking these questions the teacher must avoid any appearance of attempting to change the student's belief or of sanctioning the student's belief. The important thing is for the student to get clear about what *he* really believes.

Our tentative suggestions for helping students learn to clarify the relevancy of facts when they are making value judgments on their own are as follows:

1. Point out to students the importance of checking the relevance of significant facts.

2. Explain how one goes about checking the relevance of a fact.

3. When asking questions or initiating activities designed to check the relevancy of a fact, call attention to the function of these questions and activities.

For example, when the teacher is engaged in formulating a criterion, he should point out that this is what he is doing and he should call attention to the relationship of the criterion to the value decision and to the fact in question. That is to say, the teacher should make it clear that the criterion links the fact to the value judgment. It does this because it evaluates a class of things to which the fact belongs, and it evaluates this class of things from the same point of view as that from which the value judgment is to be made.

4. Encourage students to formulate criteria, prompting them when they run into difficulty.[3]

THE EVIDENCE CARD

One concrete device we have found to be quite helpful is what we have called the "Evidence Card." The main purpose of the Evidence Card is to summarize and organize for the student those aspects of the value analysis involved in clarifying the relevance of a fact: the value judgment, the point of view from which the value judgment is to be made, the criterion, reasons for believing the criterion, reasons for not believing the criterion, and particular or specific facts which serve as backing or evidence for the fact whose relevance is being clarified.

Although the main purpose of the Evidence Card is to clarify the relevance of a fact, our experience indicates that it may profitably be used for other purposes as well.[4] It may be used to summarize the backing or evidence for the fact; this may be useful to the student when faced with a conflict between the relevance of a fact and the adequacy of the fact. Although we have discussed these two aspects under separate tasks, in practice they are closely related. The student is often faced with trying to decide whether a purported fact, even though relevant, is really important enough to retain in the value analysis. This decision can be a difficult one when the backing for the fact is questionable, and it is helpful to have this backing directly in front of one when trying to make the decision.

The Evidence Card also serves certain practical purposes. A number of them can be moved around physically, facilitating reranking of facts or changing their valence. Discussions can be focused on the card when it is pinned on a board or put in an opaque projector.[5]

Although the teacher and students may feel that all the material relevant is too much to put on one card, we shall illustrate one way in which it can be done. Using this format as a guide, the teacher and students can decide just how much to put on a card.

The simplest form of an Evidence Card would contain the student's value judgment, his fact about the object being evaluated,[6] and the criterion the student has formulated to test the relevancy of the fact. This simple form of the Evidence Card is presented in Figure 3.[7] The example in the figure is the one discussed above. (The card itself can be a 3" x 5", 4" x 6", etc., although the size is not particularly important.)

Figure 3. **Simple Form of Evidence Card**

Value judgment: Relief is morally wrong.

Fact: Relief gives money to people who haven't earned it.

Criterion: Practices which give money to people who haven't earned it are morally wrong.

An alternative form for the Evidence Card is presented in Figure 4. It highlights the logical interrelations among the value judgment, fact, and criterion.[8] This form has the advantage of helping the student further in formulating criteria, since it facilitates the checking of whether terms are used in the same sense in both the value judgment and criterion. However for the sake of simplicity we will focus on the form presented in Figure 3.

The next step is to add a column at the right side of the card to indicate the point of view. In the example we are discussing

Figure 4. Simple Form of Evidence Card, with Interrelations
of Value Judgment, Fact, and Criterion

	VO	Characteristic	VT
Value judgment: Relief			Morally wrong
Fact:	Relief	gives money to people who haven't earned it.	
Criterion: Practices*		give money to people who haven't earned it.	Morally wrong

*Comparison Class: the class of things to which the value object belongs.

Figure 5. Simple Form of Evidence Card with Point of View

		Point of View
Value judgment:	Relief is morally wrong.	Moral
Fact:	Relief gives money to people who haven't earned it.	
Criterion:	Practices which give money to people who haven't earned it are morally wrong.	Moral

the moral point of view is the appropriate one, as indicated in Figure 5.

The next step is to place the specific evidence or backing for the fact on the *back* of the Evidence Card. (We suggest the back only because of space limitations.) Since there will often be evidence contrary to the fact, this can also be included. Figure 6 displays this step in the development. Note that the contrary statement brings up the question of what it means to "earn" money.

Finally, the reasons for and against believing the criterion

**Figure 6. Back of Evidence Card,
with Backing and Contrary Evidence for Fact**

Backing (Positive)	Contrary (Negative)
People on relief in Detroit receive $175 per month and have no jobs.	Some people on relief work hard even though they don't have a job.
People on relief in Chicago get $200 a month and do not have jobs.	

**Figure 7. Back of Evidence Card, with Backing and Contrary
Evidence for the Fact, and Reasons for and Against the Criterion**

Backing (Positive)	Contrary (Negative)
People on relief in Detroit receive $175 a month and have no jobs.	Some people on relief work hard even though they do not have a job.
People on relief in Chicago get $200 a month and do not have jobs.	
Reasons for believing criterion Such practices lower a person's dignity and self-esteem.	Reasons for not believing criterion It can't be morally wrong to raise people's standard of living when they are victims of a system over which they have no control.
Such practices keep a person from trying to improve himself.	

are placed on the *back* of the Evidence Card, below the backing for the fact. Examples of such reasons are given in Figure 7. These are, of course, only examples, and the reader may supply his own reasons for this case.

Psychologically, the Evidence Card has seemed to have several advantages.[9] (1) It gives the student something concrete to work with and focus on. (2) Each card seems to be a kind of unit of effort, so that the completion of a card seems to give the student a definite feeling of accomplishment. This seems especially true with the slower students. (3) The Evidence

Card provides an opportunity to develop a variety of inter-related capabilities in a meaningful context, and to understand how and why they are interrelated. This understanding of interrelations also helps build the student's confidence in a difficult task. (4) The student can spend as little or as much time as he wants on each card without the teacher or other students knowing how much time he spent. This saves embar-rassment and helps build the confidence of the slower students. It also facilitates individualized instruction, thereby allowing the faster student to reach his capacity. (5) Having to put things into words on a card that he knows others will see and that he will have to defend encourages greater clarity and more justifiable statements by the student. (6) The comple-tion of Evidence Cards gives the student a feeling of pride when he sees his work in front of his peers.

V. Arriving at a Tentative Value Decision

There is very little to be said about this task. In one sense it isn't a distinct task at all. It is the act of deciding or choos-ing, and is a culmination of the preceding four tasks. If the evaluator has performed these other tasks well, particularly the task of assembling facts, he should be ready to make a tentative value decision. The rules for handling complexity in assembling facts are in fact directions for bringing the evalu-ator to the point of deciding.

VI. Principle Acceptability Testing

It was pointed out in Chapter 1 that a value judgment is only rational if the evaluator can accept the value principle implied in his judgment. In the same place four tests an evalu-ator can use to determine the acceptability of a value principle were described and illustrated. These are as follows:

New Cases Test
   The value principle is explicitly formulated, then the
   evaluator considers whether or not he can accept the

judgments that follow from attempting to apply it in other cases to which it is logically relevant.

Subsumption Test

The value principle is explicitly formulated, then the evaluator attempts to assemble facts which show that the value principle is a case of some more general value principle that he accepts.

Role Exchange Test

The evaluator imaginatively exchanges roles with someone else affected by the application of the principle, then considers whether or not he can still accept the principle as it applies to him in this role.

Universal Consequences Test

The evaluator imagines what the consequences would be if everyone in similar circumstances were to engage in the action being evaluated, then considers whether or not he can accept these consequences.

We want now to consider things a teacher can do to stimulate students to apply these tests and to help them to do an adequate job of applying them. This may well be the most difficult task the teacher has in conducting a value analysis. If the aspect of ego development theory discussed below in this chapter is sound, i.e., that ego development is characterized by a number of closely interrelated functions developing in a sequence of stages, there will be a number of students who because of their stage of ego development will not recognize that value judgments are based on principles. Also there will be some students who are incapable of imagining themselves in another's circumstances. This means that some students will not be able to use all of the principle acceptability tests, and some will not be able to use any of these tests without a great deal of help from the teacher.

NEW CASES

To apply the New Cases Test one must know how to formulate the principle implied in his value judgment and he must be able to recognize cases to which the principle logically applies.

The value principle implied in a judgment may be formulated by taking the significant facts about the value object, those facts which constitute one's reasons for his value judgment, and stating that any case with these same features has the same value rating. Consider the following example. A man decides that lowering the voting age to eighteen is unwise. The facts he cites as reasons for his judgment are that eighteen-year-olds are not emotionally mature, they own little property, and are not well-informed about public issues. The value principle implied in this judgment is "It is unwise to allow anyone who is not emotionally mature, who owns little property, and who is not well-informed to vote." Notice that this principle cites the same *kinds* of facts as those given as reasons for the value decision. And it indicates that all cases in which these facts obtain must be assigned the same value as the value object.

Cases to which the principle logically applies are cases having the characteristics described in the principle. For example, the principle in the example above would apply to a forty-year-old "mama's boy" who owns nothing but his clothes and seldom reads or listens to news stories. The principle tells us it would be unwise to allow this man to vote.

The teacher may help a student apply the New Cases Test by formulating the principle he thinks is implied in the student's evaluation, then asking the student if he accepts this principle. If the student does not accept the value principle as formulated, the teacher must review the student's reasons carefully and reformulate the principle. When the student accepts the principle, the teacher proceeds to apply it to a new case and asks the student if he can accept the evaluation resulting from its application to this new case. The following example illustrates this strategem.

S. I don't think we ought to have a guaranteed annual income, because some people would be getting money without working for it. *(S. makes an evaluation and gives a reason to support it.)*

T. Do you think, then, that people ought not to get money

without working for it?*(T. formulates principle he thinks is implicit in S.'s evaluation.)*

S. Yes. *(S. affirms principle as formulated by T.)*

T. Some people inherit large amounts of money. They don't work for this money. Do you think they ought not to get it? *(T. identifies new case and asks student if he can accept the evaluation resulting from the application of the principle to this case.)*

In this strategem the teacher has formulated the principle implied in the student's judgment and has described a new case to which it applies. When a student becomes familiar with this process the teacher may require him to formulate his principle and to think of new cases to which his principle applies. Here the teacher must be prepared to help the student judge whether or not the principle formulated by the student actually is implied by his judgment and whether or not the new case really is a case to which the principle applies. This latter type of procedure should help the student develop the ability to use the New Cases Test on his own.

SUBSUMPTION TEST

Applying the Subsumption Test also requires that one be able to formulate the principle implicit in his evaluation. In addition, it requires that the evaluator be able to construct and recognize an argument in which a value principle is *validly deduced* from a more general value principle together with a set of facts.[10] The facts in such an argument must show that the class of objects being rated in the value principle belongs to the class of objects being rated in the more general value principle. Suppose we wanted to test the value principle, "It is unwise to grant voting rights to anyone who is emotionally immature and ill-informed on public issues." Using the Subsumption Test we may try to show that it is a special case of a more general value principle to the effect that it is unwise to allow voting rights to anyone who is unlikely to make a rational decision. To make this case we would have to produce facts showing that persons who are not emotionally mature and are not well-informed about public issues are not likely to make rational decisions about candidates.

To help a student apply the Subsumption Test the teacher must begin by getting an explicit formulation of the value principle implicit in the student's judgment. Ways of accomplishing this were discussed in connection with the New Cases Test. The second step is that of finding out whether or not the student has facts and a more general value principle to support his value principle. This can be accomplished by asking the student why he accepts the principle or what reasons he has for accepting the principle. If the student responds by stating facts about the class of value objects referred to in the principle, the teacher may help him formulate the more general value principle implied by these facts. If, on the other hand, the student gives a more general value principle, the teacher may ask what facts make this more general principle relevant to determining the acceptability of the value principle in question. By this sort of questioning the teacher should be able to elicit both the more general value principle and the facts which make it relevant. The final step is that of helping the student determine the validity of the argument he has given in response to the questioning. The following example illustrates this procedure.

T. You think, then, that any commercial venture which is hazardous to sea life is undesirable. *(T. formulates principle implicit in S.'s evaluation.)*

S. Yes. *(S. affirms principle as formulated by T.)*

T. Why? *(T. probes for more general principle.)*

S. Because it is a bad thing to endanger resources needed for sustaining human life. *(S. gives more general value principle.)*

T. What has that to do with regarding commercial ventures which are dangerous to sea life as undesirable? *(T. tries to elicit facts to complete the subsuming argument.)*

S. Sea life produces food and much of the oxygen that is needed to support human life.

ROLE EXCHANGE TEST

To apply the Role Exchange Test one must be able to identify persons or groups significantly affected by the action being evaluated. He must also be able to imagine himself in the same circumstances as these other persons.

There are several ways in which the teacher can aid a student in applying the exchange of roles test. He can identify a person significantly affected by the action and ask the student to consider what it would be like to be in this other person's circumstances. Consider the following example:

S. I think everyone who goes to college should be exempted from the draft.

T. Suppose you couldn't go to college because you didn't have enough money or good enough grades. Would you still feel that everyone who goes to college should be exempted from the draft?

The teacher may also help a student imagine himself in the other person's circumstances by describing in detail what the other person's circumstances are. Consider the example below:

S. It's not right to make restaurants serve Negroes if they don't want to serve them.

T. Would you still say that if you were a Negro?

S. I don't know.

T. Well, put yourself in their shoes. Suppose you went out to eat with a group of friends and the restaurant served all the rest of them but not you. Or suppose you were invited to a banquet but couldn't go because the restaurant wouldn't serve you. Think of what it would be like to stop to eat after a long day's drive and the only restaurant in town wouldn't serve you even though you had money to pay and were well-dressed.

UNIVERSAL CONSEQUENCES TEST

The Universal Consequences Test can be used only when the value object is an action. It is most relevant when the Role

Exchange Test is difficult to apply because the effects of the action *by itself* are not significant. The teacher may lead a student to apply this test by asking him to consider the consequences of everyone's engaging in the action in question. This is what the teacher does in the following example:

S. I don't see anything wrong with refusing to pay my income tax when the government is going to use it for something I don't approve of.

T. Have you considered what would happen to the government and the country if everyone refused to pay their income tax when they thought the government was going to use it for something they didn't approve of?

In some cases the student may have difficulty imagining what the consequences would be if everyone were to engage in the action. The example below illustrates how the teacher might help a student grasp these consequences.

S. I'm not sure what would happen if everyone refused to pay their income tax when they didn't like the way the government was spending it.

T. Well, we know that many people disagree with the way the government spends the taxpayers' money. In fact, I guess most of us disapprove of some government program or other. Don't you think, then, that the government might have a very difficult time getting enough money to maintain essential services such as our system of law courts, our military defense system, our highways, our state department, our health programs, etc.?

In accordance with the general hypotheses stated earlier we suggest that the teacher may help a student develop capabilities for applying these principle acceptability tests by:

1. drawing attention to the importance of testing the acceptability of the value principle implicit in one's judgment.

2. explicitly identifying as principle acceptability testing procedures those activities he initiates to get the student to test his value principle.

3. requiring the student to play an active role in initiating and carrying out activities to test the acceptability of the principle implicit in his value judgment.

VII. Implications of Ego Development Theory for the Development of Capabilities for Value Analysis

Throughout this chapter, we have offered a number of specific suggestions for achieving Objective 2, helping students develop the capabilities and dispositions required for making rational value decisions. These specific suggestions all fit one or more of the general hypotheses stated at the beginning of this chapter. These hypotheses involved such teacher activities as actively engaging the students in operations, increasing the student's responsibilities in value analyses, pointing out what task is accomplished by various operations, and calling attention to the importance of any given task in terms of how it meets the standards of rational evaluation.

In trying to formulate teaching strategies for value analysis, the teacher may take into account a variety of principles of learning and individual student characteristics such as current knowledge, interest in subject, readiness, etc. The above suggestions for developing capabilities for value analysis, for example, take into account such factors as the gradual learning of independence in complex tasks, the pacing of effort in complex tasks, the awareness of the importance of a task as a motivational factor, and the student perceiving the teacher as a model in difficult tasks.

In a sense, the suggestions and hypotheses offered to this point are based on rather common sense and general beliefs about how students might develop capabilities of almost any sort. These beliefs have been tested in a wide variety of contexts — including laboratory and classroom — with a wide variety of phenomena. Since they have been tested so widely for so long they have acquired the status of common sense beliefs. Since these common sense beliefs provide the teacher with good reasons for teaching strategies for almost any subject matter or objective, it seems quite reasonable to use these beliefs and strategies in developing capabilities for value analysis.

In addition to using common beliefs, the teacher may also want to use a systematic body of theory or research as a basis for formulating his teaching strategies to develop capabilities for value analysis. Such a systematic body of psychological theory or research would presumably provide the teacher with sound and specific reasons for such teaching strategies. However, although there are a variety of theories and research findings of at least some relevance in helping formulate teaching strategies for value analysis, it is our judgment that most of these theories and research findings lack any substantial implications that could be described here.

The one exception we have found to this judgment is a loosely organized body of theory we shall call ego development theory (after Loevinger, 1966, 1969). Our two main reasons for discussing ego development theory and its implications for formulating teaching strategies to develop capabilities for value analysis may be stated briefly as follows. (1) The tasks to be performed in a value analysis are similar to the interrelated functions in ego development theory, as will be discussed below. (2) Ego development theorists have done a great deal of research in values and value-related phenomena. Thus the development of capabilities for value analysis is very likely to be an integral aspect of ego development. We will state one of the most essential ideas of the theory, indicate briefly some of the general implications for formulating teaching strategies to develop capabilities for value analysis, and suggest some ways to identify a student's stage of ego development.

I. EGO DEVELOPMENT THEORY

Ego development theorists[11] disagree on a number of points, but do agree on one essential idea that is important for our purposes, namely that *ego development is characterized by a number of closely interrelated functions which develop in a sequence of stages.* What the theorists disagree on, then, are such matters as the number and kind of functions, and the number and kind of stages in the developmental sequence.

With respect to the number and variety of *functions*, for example, Loevinger (1966) focuses on impulse control, character development, interpersonal style, and conscious preoccupations. Kohlberg (1969), concentrating on the moral aspects of ego development, includes value, choice, sanctions and motives, rules, rights and authority, positive justice, and punitive justice. With respect to the number and variety of *stages*, on the other hand, the similarities and differences are best summarized in Figure 8 (from Kohlberg, 1969), which compares and integrates the stages of a number of ego development theorists.

Regardless of the exact number or nature of the stages, the stages have the following general characteristics: (1) The stages form an invariable order or succession in development. (2) No stage can be skipped. (3) The stages are qualitatively different, in the sense that for any of the diverse functions its mode of functioning or operating is different from stage to stage. (4) At each stage, the diverse functions are a "structured whole": i.e., each of the diverse functions represents an underlying organization which characterizes that stage. (5) Each stage is more complex than the preceding one, and is a hierarchical integration of the preceding stage. Thus each stage is based on and transforms the preceding stage, and at the same time prepares for the next stage.

The chart in Figure 9 illustrates the essential idea of interrelated functions developing in a sequence of stages. The chart contains six interrelated functions at each of four stages of ego development. The four stages are from Figure 8 and the six functions are from three sources: Loevinger (1966) for conscious preoccupations, interpersonal style, and rules; Kohlberg (1969) for orientation to intentions and consequences, and motives for moral action; and Kaplan and Crockett (1968) for modes of conflict resolution.

Figure 8. Summary of Stages Described by Ego Development Theorists (from Kohlberg, 1969)*

Author	Amoral	1. Fearful-Dependent	2. Opportunistic	3. Conforming to Persons	4. Conforming to Rule	5,6. Principled-Autonomous
			Moral Stages			
McDougall (1908)	1. instinctive		2. reward and punishment	3. anticipation of praise and blame		4. regulation by an internal ideal
J. M. Baldwin (1906)		1. adualistic	2. intellectual		3. ideal	
L. Hobhouse (1906)	1. instinctive	2. obligation as magical taboo		3. obligation as ideals of personal virtue	4. obligation as rules of society	5. rational ethical principles
Piaget (1948)	1. premoral	2. heteronomous obedience to adult authority	3. autonomous reciprocity and equality oriented			4. autonomous—ideal reciprocity and equality
Peck and Havighurst (1960)	1. amoral		2. expedient	3. conforming	4. irrational-conscientious	5. rational-altruistic
Kohlberg (1958)		1. obedience & punishment oriented	2. instrumental egoism and exchange	3. good-boy approval oriented	4. authority, rule and social order oriented	5. social contract legalist orientation 6. moral principle orientation
			Ego or Character Types			
Fromm (1955) Riesman (1950)		1. receptive, tradition-directed	2. exploitative, anomic	3. marketing, other-directed	4. hoarding, inner-directed	5. productive, autonomous
C. Sullivan, Grant and Grant (1957)		I_2 passive-demanding	I_3 conformist (exploitative)	I_3 conformist (cooperative)	I_4 authoritarian—guilty	I_6 self-consistent I_7 integrative
Harvey, Hunt & Schroder (1961)		1. absolutistic-evaluative	2. self-differentiating	3. empathic		4. integrated-independent
Loevinger (1966)	1. presocial	2. impulse-ridden, fearful	3. expedient	4. conformist	5. conscientious	6. autonomous 7. integrated

* Reprinted from "Stage and Sequence: the Cognitive Developmental Approach to Socialization" by L. Kohlberg in D. A. Goslin, *Handbook of Socialization Theory and Research.* Chicago: Rand McNally, 1969. By permission of the publisher.

STAGES

EGO FUNCTIONS

STAGES	Conscious Preoccupation	Interpersonal Style	Rules	Orientation to Intentions and Consequences	Motives for Moral Action	Modes of Conflict Resolution
Opportunistic	Control and advantage, domination, deception, getting the better of life is a zero-sum game.	Exploitive, manipulative, shift away from dependence.	Obeyed in terms of immediate advantage.	Focus on the instrumental value of an act in serving a need, and ignores label and physical consequences.	Action motivated by desire for reward or benefit. Possible guilt reactions ignored. Punishment viewed in pragmatic manner.	Aggregation, univalence, denial, rejection of task.
Conforming to Persons	Material things. Status and reputation, appearance, adjustment.	Genuine interpersonal reciprocity, mutual trust extended only to narrow in-groups, seen mainly in terms of actions rather than feelings or motives.	Obeyed because they are the rules, partially internalized.	Action evaluated according to the type of person or motive involved in the act. Circumstances may justify deviant action.	Action motivated by anticipation of disapproval of others, real or imagined.	Univalence through linguistic reinterpretation. Resolution through grossly differentiated sources.
Conforming to Rules	Obligations, ideals, traits, and achievement as measured by inner standards rather than just recognition.	Seen in terms of feelings and traits rather than actions. Cherishing of conflicting demands, renunciation of unattainable.	Morality has been internalized. Inner moral imperatives take place over group-sanctioned rules.	An act is always or categorically wrong, regardless of motives or circumstances, if it violates a rule and does foreseeable harm to others.	Action motivated by anticipation of dishonor, i.e., institutionalized blame for failure of duty, and by guilt over concrete harm done to others.	
Autonomous-Integrated	Role differentiation, individuality, not self-fulfillment. Integrated identity.	Intensive recognition of inevitable mutual interdependence. Recognition of others' need for autonomy (toleration). Cherishing of individual differences.	Coping with conflict. Reconciliation of conflicting demands, renunciation of unattainable.	End doesn't justify means, although the circumstances or motive may modify disapproval. Act is right if it follows from general self-chosen principles.	Concern about respect of self and community (where based on reason, not emotion). Concern to avoid self being irrational, inconsistent, non-purposive. Concern about self-condemnation for violating own principle.	Differentiation. Transcendence.

Figure 9. Six Ego Functions for Four Stages of Ego Development

II. Implications of Ego Development Theory
   for Value Analysis

Three implications of ego development theory for value analysis will be discussed briefly. The first involves the expectations the teacher can reasonably hold for the student's capability of performing a rational value analysis. The second involves the kind of teacher control over what the student does in a value analysis. The third involves the way groups are formed for group discussions.

A. Ego Development and Expectations for Rational Value Judgments. The six tasks to be carried out in a value analysis, i.e., identifying and clarifying the value question, assembling purported facts, assessing the truth of purported facts, etc., are very similar to some of the important functions included explicitly in ego development theory, such as the interpreting, formulating, and justifying of intentions and consequences, the formulating and justifying of motives for moral action, and the interpreting of and conforming to rules. Other functions that play a less prominent but still an important part in value analysis are role-taking, conscious preoccupations, interpersonal style, and modes of conflict resolution.

It seems plausible, then, to assume that the interrelated functions in ego development are similar to and include as special cases the capabilities for carrying out the tasks in a value analysis. Thus, the development of capabilities for value analysis is an integral aspect of ego development. The implication of this conclusion is that the student's capabilities for conducting a value analysis will depend upon his stage of ego development. Thus, the capability for formulating a fully rational value judgment is — according to ego development theory — achieved only at the *highest* stage of ego development.[12]

The teacher can expect a student at the highest stage of ego development, then, to be capable of carrying out tasks in a value analysis so as to meet the standards for a rational value judgment. What can the teacher expect from a student at the lower stages of ego development? The description of the "concrete individual" — an individual at one of the lower stages of ego development — by Harvey (1969),[13] based on considerable research, suggests a number of ways such an individual would perform in a value analysis. Harvey points out that the "concrete individual" has a greater tendency to polarize evaluations, greater dependence on social areas related to role and status as guides to judgment, need for cognitive consistency and greater change from the experience of cognitive dissonance, more stereotyping in complex and changing problems of high involvement, poorer delineation of means and ends, paucity of problem-solving methods, and poorer capacity to act "as if" and assume various roles.

Let us indicate briefly how such an individual might perform in each of the six tasks in value analysis discussed earlier in the chapter. In identifying and clarifying the value question, he might perceive the question as more polarized than it actually is, and be likely to formulate the question in a rather stereotyped way. In assembling purported facts, he might restrict his range of purported facts gathered and restrict them essentially to one valence, both of these because of his need for cognitive consistency. He might also have considerable trouble in distinguishing means from ends. In assessing the truth of purported facts, he might give more weight to sources of high status. In clarifying the relevance of facts, he might have considerable difficulty giving relevance to facts of both positive and negative valence and to facts reflecting more than one or two concerns. In arriving at a tentative value judgment, he might polarize his value judgments, being unable to consider such qualified judgments as "fairly detrimental" and "somewhat desirable" and might use such value terms as "intolerable" rather than "desirable." In testing the acceptability of his principle,[14] he might have difficulty in assuming another role in the role exchange test.

B. Teacher Control in Value Analysis. Schroder and Harvey (1963) distinguish unilateral from interdependent conditions. In unilateral conditions, the teacher presents the student with ways of evaluating and responding to situations without the student's having the opportunity to explore and generate these ways for himself. The emphasis is on the student matching and reproducing what the teacher gives him, with rewards and punishments depending on this matching. The search for criteria that are independent of the teacher comes to be viewed very negatively by the student.

Interdependent conditions are those in which the teacher allows the student the freedom to participate in developing his own ways of evaluating and responding to situations. The student is rewarded for looking and exploring, so that specific behaviors and responses to a situation are not particularly important.

The problem for the teacher, then, is to arrange the conditions of a value analysis so that it is as interdependent as is optimal for each student *at his stage of development*.[15] Consider two examples. (1) Schroder and Harvey (1963) suggest that if the student is still at one of the lower stages where he relies heavily on a normative structure (parents, church, teacher, etc.) the teacher can encourage autonomy within the normative structure. If the teacher is or represents the normative structure for the student, encouraging autonomy within the normative structure is easier. With other normative structures (parents, church, etc.), the teacher, by knowing the normative structure well, might help the student by getting him to clarify and represent faithfully the normative structure. With respect to the tasks in a value analysis, the teacher might encourage autonomy in the following ways. In identifying and clarifying the value question, the normative structure would probably dictate the specific value judgment. The teacher can encourage the student to be clear on the point of view represented in the value judgment of the normative structure and how the value judgment from this point of view differs from the value judgments that can be made from points of view other than that of the normative structure, and can also encourage the student to seek detail about the value object that is not specified by the normative structure. In assembling purported facts, the normative structure would probably dictate what facts are to be considered and what valence they have. The teacher can encourage the student to be clear about the ranking of facts and the concerns they represent within the normative structure, and to add and rank facts which do not conflict with the normative structure. In assessing the truth of the purported facts, the normative structure would probably dictate what is true and what isn't. The teacher can encourage the student to assess the truth of the purported facts he has added in the previous task, i.e., purported facts on which the normative structure has nothing to say. In the remaining tasks, the teacher might try formulating criteria for the facts added which do not conflict with the normative structure. However, there may not be much more the teacher can do, since this would very likely arouse too much conflict between the student and the normative structure. The use of the Rudimentary Procedure described in Chapter 3 might be especially suited for students at this stage, since it allows the teacher to encourage autonomy and carry out the above suggestions and involves no explicit work with criteria and principles. The latter is important, since students at this concrete stage have considerable difficulty with abstract criteria and principles.

(2) Schroder and Harvey (1963) also suggest that for the student who is at the next stage, reacting against a normative structure, the teacher can encourage the student to be highly autonomous with low normative pressure. If the teacher is or represents the normative structure for the student, the teacher can encourage the student to be autonomous from him. In general, there is much opportunity for the student to be autonomous within both the Rudimentary Procedure and the Extended Procedure described in Chapter 3, for example in listing as many positive and negative statements as he wants, ranking them the way he wants, and finding as many causes and solutions as he wants. Further, normative pressure is rather low since only simple and reasonable "logical" and procedural rules are involved in the procedures. (Even these can be deemphasized if necessary.) More specifically, with respect to the tasks in a value analysis, the teacher can encourage the student to be highly autonomous in the following ways. In identifying and clarifying the value question, the

teacher can encourage the student to justify a value judgment opposite to that of the normative structure, or to work on causes and solutions to negative aspects of the normative structure, or to take points of view very different from that of the normative structure. In assembling purported facts, the teacher can encourage the student to collect many facts not considered by the normative structure or facts of opposite valence to those considered acceptable by the normative structure. In assessing the truth of purported facts, the teacher can encourage the student to examine the different ways there are of assessing truth, and relate these to how the normative structure assesses truth. In clarifying relevance of the facts by formulating criteria and in formulating and testing value principles, the teacher can formulate a variety of these for the student — the student will still experience difficulty with abstract criteria and principles at this stage, which is still rather concrete — and allow or encourage autonomy in selecting those which oppose the normative structure.

C. Formation of Groups for Group Discussions. Turiel (1966) and Blatt (1969) have indicated that students at a given stage, say stage N, can understand the arguments of all stages below their own and also can understand the arguments of students at stages one higher than their own, i.e., stage N + 1, but cannot understand the arguments of students or the teacher at stage N + 2. According to these results, then, one would not expect students at, e.g., the Opportunistic stage (see Figure 9), to be able to understand the arguments, criteria, and principles of students at the Conforming to Rules or Autonomous-Integrated stages, but they (Opportunistic students) would be able to understand and even try to imitate or model students at the Conforming to Persons stage. There might even be overt hostility, not just lack of understanding, on the part of stage N students toward stage N + 2 or higher students. The teacher might be on the lookout for such phenomena, and modify his teaching strategies accordingly, e.g., by forming the discussion groups so that each group has only stage N and stage N + 1 students.

III. ASSESSING A STUDENT'S STAGE OF EGO DEVELOPMENT

We suggest three ways of assessing a student's stage of ego development. The first involves an informal judgment based on the teacher's general observations of a variety of the student's behavior relevant to the ego development stages. Since the chart in Figure 9 provides a general guide to the kinds of interrelated functions at the different stages of development, the use of this chart by the teacher in identifying students at the different stages would illustrate this first way of assessing stages.

The second way of assessing a student's stage of ego development is also informal, but is based specifically on the teacher's observations of the student's performance during a value analysis. Some suggestions are inherent in the chart in Figure 9, such as the judging of acts in terms of intentions or consequences. Our discussion above of how the "concrete individual" might perform in a value analysis suggested a number of observations the teacher might make.

The third way of assessing a student's stage of ego development is to use one of the tests constructed for the purpose of measuring ego development or some aspect of it. Examples of such tests may be found in Loevinger and Wessler (1968) and Wessler and Loevinger (1968), in Harvey (1969), in Hunt and Halverson (1964), and in Kohlberg (1958).[16]

NOTES

[1] For an extensive discussion of this technique for clarifying terms see John Wilson, *Thinking with Concepts* (Cambridge: Cambridge University Press, 1963).

[2] Cues for distinguishing factual from evaluative assertions were discussed in the first section of Chapter 1. Another useful and very readable discussion of this distinction is to be found in John Wilson, *Language and the Pursuit of Truth* (Cambridge: Cambridge University Press, 1958), pp. 22-28.

[3] See Chapter 3 for a treatment of how to teach students to formulate criteria.

[4] One such purpose is in the Extended Procedure described in Chapter 3.

[5] We have incorporated this use in the Extended Procedure described in Chapter 3.

[6] In Chapter 3, we use the term "Description" to refer to a fact or purported fact about the value object.

[7] The Evidence Card used in the Extended Procedure described in Chapter 3 is basically this simple form.

[8] This form is similar to the chart in Figure 18 in Chapter 3.

[9] Several of these advantages are similar to advantages of the Fact-Assembly Chart.

[10] Readers who wish to learn more about valid deductive arguments will find a useful treatment of this topic in Robert H. Ennis, *Ordinary Logic* (Englewood Cliffs, N.J.: Prentice-Hall, Inc., 1969).

[11] The best known are Freud (certain parts, e.g. 1955) and Piaget (Piaget and Inhelder, 1969; Furth, 1969). Others are Sullivan (1953), Werner (1957), Kohlberg (1969), Harvey, Hunt, and Schroder (1961), Peck and Havighurst (1960), Erikson (1950, 1959), Isaacs (1956), Sullivan, Grant, and Grant (1957), and Stierlin (1968).

[12] It is interesting to note that two ego development theorists actually use the term "rational" in some way to designate the top stage (Peck and Havighurst, 1960; Hobhouse, 1906), and other ego development theorists use such related terms as "principled" and "autonomous."

[13] See also Harvey and Schroder (1963, p. 116).

[14] If he were even able to consider that value judgments are based on principles.

[15] Note the similarity of this implication to Hypothesis 1 stated at the beginning of this chapter (regarding the increase of student responsibility for carrying out the tasks in a value analysis).

[16] A study by Sullivan, McCullough, and Stager (1970) reports intercorrelations of three of these tests on a sample of adolescents.

SELECTED READINGS
IN VALUATIVE TEACHING STRATEGIES

Moore, W. Edgar. *Creative and Critical Thinking.* Boston: Houghton Mifflin Company, 1967.

National College of Education. *Value Sharing.* Evanston, Illinois: National College of Education, 1969.

Oliver, Donald W., and James P. Shaver. *Teaching Public Issues in the High School.* Boston: Houghton Mifflin Company, 1966.

Raths, Louis E., Merrill Harmin, and Sidney B. Simon. *Values and Teaching.* Columbus, Ohio: Charles E. Merrill Publishing Co., 1966.

Scriven, Michael. "Student Values as Educational Objectives," *Proceedings of the 1965 Invitational Conference on Testing Problems,* pp. 33-49. Princeton, New Jersey: Educational Testing Service, 1966.

Smith, B. Othanel. "Teaching and Testing Values," *Proceedings of the 1965 Invitational Conference on Testing Problems,* pp. 50-59. Princeton, New Jersey: Educational Testing Service, 1966.

REFERENCES AND READINGS
IN EGO DEVELOPMENT THEORY

Blatt, M. "The Effects of Classroom Discussion Programs upon Children's Level of Moral Judgment." Unpublished doctoral dissertation, University of Chicago, 1969.

Erikson, E. H. *Childhood and Society*. New York: Norton, 1950.

Erikson, E. H. "Identity and the Life Cycle," *Psychological Issues*, 1959, 1, Whole No. 1.

Freud, S. *Beyond the Pleasure Principle*. Vol. XVIII. (Standard edition.) London: The Hogarth Press Ltd., 1955, pp. 7-64. (First printed in 1920.)

Furth, H. G. *Piaget and Knowledge*. Englewood Cliffs, New Jersey: Prentice-Hall, 1969.

Harvey, O. J. "Belief Systems and Education: Some Implications for Change." Unpublished paper presented at a conference on "The Role of Affect in Learning" at Salishan, Oregon.

Harvey, O. J., and H. M. Schroder. "Cognitive Aspects of Self and Motivation." In O. J. Harvey (ed.), *Motivation and Social Interaction*. New York: Ronald Press, 1963. Pp. 95-133.

Hobhouse, L. T. *Morals in Evolution*. London: Chapman and Hall, 1906.

Hunt, D. E. "A Conceptual Systems Change Model and Its Application to Education." In O. J. Harvey (ed.), *Experience, Structure, and Adaptability*. New York: Springer, 1966. Pp. 277-302.

Hunt, D. E., and C. Halverson. "Manual for Scoring Sentence Completion Responses for Adolescents." Unpublished scoring manual, Syracuse University, 1964.

Isaacs, K. S. "Relatability, a Proposed Construct and an Approach to Its Validation." Unpublished doctoral dissertation, University of Chicago, 1956.

Kaplan, B., and W. H. Crockett. "Developmental Analysis of Modes of Resolution." Chapter in R. P. Abelson (ed.), *Theories of Cognitive Consistency: A Sourcebook*. Chicago: Rand McNally, 1968. Pp. 661-669.

Kohlberg, L. "The Development of Modes of Moral Thinking and Choice in the Years 10 to 16." Unpublished doctoral dissertation, University of Chicago, 1958.

Kohlberg, L. "Stage and Sequence: the Cognitive-Developmental Approach to Socialization." In D. A. Goslin (ed.), *Handbook of Socialization Theory and Research*. Chicago: Rand McNally, 1969. Pp. 347-480.

Loevinger, Jane. "The Meaning and Measurement of Ego Development," *American Psychologist*, 1966, 21, pp. 195-217.

Loevinger, Jane. "Theories of Ego Development." In L. Breger (ed.), *Clinical-Cognitive Psychology*. Englewood Cliffs, New Jersey: Prentice-Hall, 1969. Pp. 83-135.

Loevinger, J., and R. Wessler. "Measuring Ego Development by Sentence Completions, I: Theoretical and Methodological Issues." Paper presented to the American Psychological Association, San Francisco, August 31, 1968.

Mehrabian, A. "Cognitive-Developmental Approaches to Personality." Chapter 5 in *An Analysis of Personality Theories*. Englewood Cliffs, New Jersey: Prentice-Hall, 1968. Pp. 121-164.

Peck, R. F., and R. J. Havighurst. *The Psychology of Character Development*. New York: Wiley, 1960.

Piaget, J., and Bärbel Inhelder. *The Psychology of the Child*. New York: Basic Books, 1969.

Schroder, H. M., and O. J. Harvey. "Conceptual Organization and Group Structure." In O. J. Harvey (ed.), *Motivation and Social Interaction.* New York: Ronald Press, 1963. Pp. 134-166.

Stierlin, Helm. *Conflict and Reconciliation.* Garden City, N.Y.: Doubleday (Anchor), 1968.

Sullivan, Edmund V., George McCullough, and Mary Stager. "A Developmental Study of the Relationship Between Conceptual, Ego, and Moral Development," *Child Development,* Vol. 41, No. 2, June, 1970, pp. 399-411.

Sullivan, C., Marguerite Q. Grant, and J. D. Grant. "The Development of Interpersonal Maturity: Applications of Delinquency," *Psychiatry,* 1957, 20, pp. 373-385.

Sullivan, H. S. *The Interpersonal Theory of Psychiatry.* New York: Norton, 1953.

Turiel, E. "An Experimental Test of the Sequentiality of Developmental Stages in the Child's Moral Judgment," *Journal of Personality and Social Psychology,* 1966, 3, pp. 611-618.

Werner, H. "The Conception of Development from a Comparative and Organismic Point of View." In D. Harris (ed.), *The Concept of Development.* Minneapolis: University of Minnesota Press, 1957. Pp. 125-148.

Wessler, R., and J. Loevinger. "Measuring Ego Development by Sentence Completions, II: Empirical Evaluations of the Interpretive Scheme." Paper presented to the American Psychological Association, San Francisco, August 31, 1968.

3

Procedures
for Value Analysis

JAMES CHADWICK AND MILTON MEUX

☐ In Chapter 2 we discussed a variety of tasks in value analysis and indicated a variety of techniques a teacher could employ both to help the students make the most rational value judgment they can about the value object in question (Objective 1) and to help the students develop capabilities for making rational value judgments (Objective 2). Our discussion left open many decisions to the teacher, such as the amount and kind of effort on each task, the order in which he wants the students to pursue the tasks, and the extent and kind of his own participation in the value analysis. Thus, although we made many specific suggestions to the teacher, these suggestions in no way constitute a specific procedure for the teacher to follow step by step through a value analysis.

In this chapter, then, we turn to a description of two teaching procedures — the Rudimentary Procedure and the Extended Procedure — which we have developed and tried in the classroom with considerable success. We describe also two pictorial models of value analysis which form the basis of the procedures, and a method for progressing from the Rudimentary Procedure to the Extended Procedure.

Two comments will help the reader in this chapter. (1) The role of the teacher in these procedures is one of consultant and advisor rather than a dispenser of information and answers.

However, this role does not preclude the use of the techniques and strategies discussed in Chapter 2. (2) The examples of actual students' work used in the chapter contain a variety of inadequacies which we could have corrected or at least have pointed out. However, we did not think this was necessary, considering that there would be some advantage to maintaining the actual "flavor" of the students' work and to providing the teacher an opportunity to judge for himself what inadequacies are present.

Rudimentary Procedure

STEP 1. *Selection of Topic.* The scope of the topic should take into account the amount of time allowed for study. For example, if only two days were available for study, then the topic should be rather limited — certainly something much less than the "Problems of the American Cities."

STEP 2. *Provision of Adequate Source Materials.* The teacher may not, and perhaps should not, obtain the material for the students; rather, he should make the students aware of where materials can be acquired. Furthermore, it is the teacher's responsibility to keep abreast of the subject so that appropriate materials can be suggested to meet the needs of each individual student.

STEP 3. *Provision of Proper Atmosphere.* Students should be allowed to discuss any aspect of the topic with their fellow students or the teacher as long as they do not infringe upon the rights of their fellow students.[1] They should be encouraged to search for information outside the school premises.

STEP 4. *Listing and Ranking Positive and Negative Statements.* The student lists positive and negative statements about the topic and then ranks statements in the order of importance to him. This step requires the students to look at both sides of the topic, and usually helps them to see issues in a clearer perspective. We have found it useful to have each student make up folders for this and most of the following steps.

Figure 1 presents the folder of an actual student who has listed and ranked positive statements and negative statements about crime.

STEP 5. *Class Discussions.* The class discusses the positive and negative statements about the topic. The method or type of discussion used here is much less important than the involvement of the students in the discussion. They should begin to feel the importance of the topic; and if enough of them do not feel it, then the teacher should examine the topic more closely. Perhaps what stimulates the teacher's sense of importance of the topic has not been communicated to the students. Whether this is the case or not, immediate steps should be taken to rectify the problem. The net result of the discussion should be a class listing of positive and negative aspects of the topic in order of their importance.

STEP 6. *Formulation of Possible Solutions.* The students formulate possible solutions for the high priority negative statements on the topic. The points made about source material and atmosphere for study in steps two and three also apply here. The student lists positive and negative statements about each possible solution.

Figure 2 presents the second folder of the student. The student has listed positive and negative statements about *each* possible solution. The possible solutions themselves are also ranked in order of their importance to the student.

STEP 7. *Question and Answer Period.* The class has a question and answer period either with the teacher or, preferably, a guest speaker. This is not a lecture period, but rather a time when the students can ask questions of an expert, expecting reliable answers.

STEP 8. *Observations and Recommendations.* In the final step the students formulate observations and recommendations, which are prepared in written form and handed in. Observations are basically all significant things the student has learned in going through the first seven steps. Recommendations, on the other hand, are things the student suggests be implemented.

Figure 3 contains Observations and Recommendations made on the basis of the contents of the folders in Figure 1 and 2.

Comment on Rudimentary Procedure. In our experience, the main usefulness of this Rudimentary Procedure is in giving the teacher the basic steps from which he can introduce his own variations and also work into the Extended Procedure.

Figure 1. **Student's folder: Listing and Ranking
of Positive and Negative Statements about Crime**

TOPIC: CRIME

Negative	Positive
1. Negroes make up 12% of the nations population and commit 53% of the crimes.	1. More jails and prisons are Inhabited by drunks and vagrants than by thieves, murders, etc.
2. Destroys property and kills.	2. Law enforcement agencies are doing good jobs.
3. Crime is increasing 6% faster than the nation's population.	3. Prison population is declining.
4. Cloggs courts.	4. Proposal on regulation of fire arms.
5. High amounts of money are needed to solve crime.	5. Organized crime is no worse than in past years.
6. Makes life miserable for everyone.	6. Provides jobs for citizens.
7. Courts are too easy.	7. F.B.I.
8. Too many types of crimes.	8. C.I.A.
9. Wire-tapping illegal.	9. Creates need for enforcement of law.
10. Not enough law enforcers.	10. Drug addiction is not increasing and does not cause crime.
11. Lack of equipment used to combat crime.	11. More small crimes than those of violence.
12. Court decisions opposite of police views.	12. Crime is not caused by lawlessness but by population increase in the 14-29 age group.
13. People (common citizens) just don't care.	(The last 6 are not in order)
(The last 7 are not in order)	

Figure 2. Student's folder: Listing and Ranking of Positive and
Negative Statements about Each of His Proposed *Solutions* for Crime

---

SOLUTION 1: OPEN HOUSING

Negative

1. Take away the privilege of selling to whom you want.
2. White citizens rebell (more discrimination).
3. Maybe white citizens would start rioting, luting, etc.

Positive

1. Give negroes a chance to live where they want.
2. Cut down on lawlessness.
3. Change the attitude of negroes.
4. Living conditions would Improve. (slums, ghetto, etc. Improve.)

SOLUTION 2: MAKE MORE & BETTER JOBS AVAILABLE

Negative

1. Take away jobs of white citizens.
2. White citizens not wanting to work with negroes.
3. More discrimination.
4. White citizens will not hire negroes.

Positive

1. Negroes can earn their living instead of stealing for it.
2. Cut down on amount of welfare aid.
3. Living conditions would Improve.
4. Education would be easier to obtain.

SOLUTION 3: INTEGRATE SCHOOLS

Negative

1. White students and parents would put up a fuss.
2. Fighting and discrimination would exist in the schools.

Positive

1. Education conditions would better.
2. Less rebelling and rioting on the negroes part.
3. Attitudes of negro children would be better.

SOLUTION 4: MORE EDUCATION

Negative

1. Negroes could not afford to pay the fees.

Positive

1. Jobs easier to obtain.
2. Able to better their environment
   a. better housing
   b. better living conditions
3. Since negroes would be able to better themselves, there would be a great decrease in rioting and discrimination.
4. Negroes would feel equal to white citizens.

Figure 3. Folder Listing Observations and Recommendations

OBSERVATIONS

1 — It will be difficult to improve the negro's environment because in so doing you infringe upon the environmental rights of white citizens.

2 — The whites hold the keys to the solution to the problem, but too many of them refuse to use them or even allow others to do so.

3 — I discovered that I am settled against crime and racism to the point that I am somewhat incapable of appreciating the Negro plight. However, this has forced me to recognize my own prejudices as well as the prejudices of my fellow citizens.

4 — It will take a long time to solve this particular problem.

RECOMMENDATIONS

1 — Improve Negro education so that the younger generations might have a more equal opportunity to make money. Money basically would improve all of the conditions in relationship to crime, that is.

2 — Big business should have more on-the-job-training programs to economically improve the negro lot so that he won't have to commit crime to live.

Pictorial Models of Evaluation

Although the Rudimentary Procedure provides the teacher with a number of specific steps he can go through, it does not provide him with any rationale for the steps. The teacher could, of course, develop his own rationale on the basis of our work in Chapters 1 and 2, and we certainly encourage the teacher to do this. However, we have found that it is helpful to keep in mind the pictorial model that was used in developing the Extended Procedure which forms the main part of this chapter.

In this section, then, we present two pictorial models. A number of points can be made about the models. (1) The models provide a link between the earlier chapters, especially Chapter 1, and specific teaching procedures. (2) The models describe some of the logical aspects of evaluation, not the psychological aspects. (3) Although the models were developed somewhat independently of the material in Chapter 1, several of the conditions or standards for rationality are incorporated in the Extended Model — such as the valence of facts (Positive and Negative in the model), necessity of the value principle and value judgment being consistent, and the necessity of both a fact and a corresponding criterion to support a value judgment (the vertical and lower horizontal lines in the model). (4) The models by themselves *can* be used directly in a discussion, and serve as a focus for the discussion, a device to "key on." We have tried both pictorial models in various contexts, but find that slower students have trouble with them.[2]

I. THE SIMPLE VALUE MODEL

The Simple Value Model has four elements. The first element is the thing being evaluated, which usually is called the value object (VO). Literally anything can be evaluated, so that the VO can be any content. The second element is the term, the value term (VT), which is applied to the value object to make the value judgment.[3] A wide variety of VTs are used — good, desirable, right, just, fair, advisable, etc. The third element is the description (D). In the description, characteristics of the

VO relevant to the VT are given, such as origins, consequences, features, etc. The fourth element is the criterion (C), some rule or standard by which it is judged whether or not the VT applies to the VO. The D and C *together* support the value judgment.[4]

These elements, along with some of the important relations among them, can be represented schematically as in Figure 4.

Figure 4. The Simple Value Model

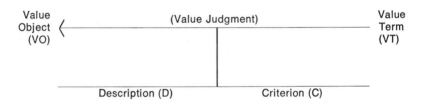

The upper horizontal line, an arrow, represents the application of the value term (VT) to the value object (VO), constituting the value judgment. The lower horizontal line over both the description (D) and the criterion (C) is to represent the fact that the description and criterion must *both* be present to provide support for the value judgment. (Description is placed on the side of the value object as a reminder that it refers to the value object.) The vertical line represents the support of the value judgment more specifically. The vertical line is put in to represent the fact that the value judgment is like a conclusion in an argument.

Let us turn, then, to an illustration of the model from an area of increasing concern, environmental pollution. Suppose that we want to support the value judgment that air pollution is undesirable. In Figure 5, "air pollution" is the value object (VO) and "undesirable" is the value term (VT), so that the value judgment is "Air pollution is undesirable." The description (D) in this case — selected from the variety of facts about the effect of air pollution — is "Air pollution contributes to emphysema." The criterion (C) here is "Any condition which contributes to emphysema is undesirable."

Figure 5. Example of the Use of the Simple Value Model
in Evaluating Air Pollution

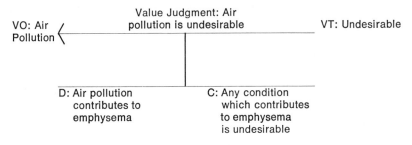

The logical aspects of the Simple Value Model can be seen more clearly, perhaps, by arranging the criterion, the description, and the value judgment in the form of a deductive argument. This is done for the example of air pollution in Figure 6.

Figure 6. The Logical Elements of the Simple Value Model
Exhibited as a Deductive Argument

Criterion ("Major Premise"):	Any condition which contributes to emphysema is undesirable
Description ("Minor Premise"):	Air pollution (a condition) contributes to emphysema
Ratio ("Conclusion"):	Air pollution is undesirable

The four basic elements (VO, VT, D, and C) of the Simple Value Model together comprise a basic and in a sense an "ideal" form of evaluation. However, the Simple Model is somewhat limited when trying to represent the typical evaluations in real life, e.g., in the classroom, which are likely to be much more complex. Even if just one VO is involved, such evaluations will typically include more than one VT, D, and C.

II. THE EXTENDED VALUE MODEL

The Simple Value Model can be extended, however, so as to describe evaluations, such as in discussions, with more than one VO, more than one VT — separating positive and negative

VTs — and a number of D-C combinations. We shall now show how the Simple Value Model may be extended to what we will call the Extended Value Model.[5] Perhaps this is best understood if introduced in a number of steps.

1. More than one support element[6] for the value judgment may be represented, as in Figure 7. Any number of support elements may be included on the line, and the line may be of any length.

Figure 7. Extension to More than One Support Element

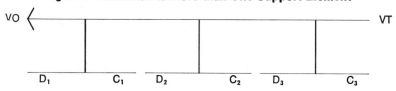

Thus a number of Ds may be relevant to the value judgment, each with an appropriate C.

2. Both positive and negative VTs may be represented by placing the positive VT on one side of the VO and the negative VT on the other side of the VO. In Figure 8, the positive VT is to the right of the VO, and the negative VT is to the left of the VO. (It is assumed that the VTs are "opposites," e.g., "good" and "bad.") The negative value judgment is also portrayed as having more than one support element.

Figure 8. Extension to Both Positive and Negative VTs

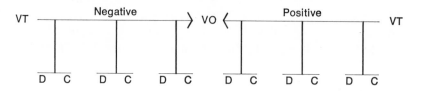

An example of the use of the Extended Value Model is presented in Figure 9. The student is evaluating Sex Education, and has three positive and three negative support elements.

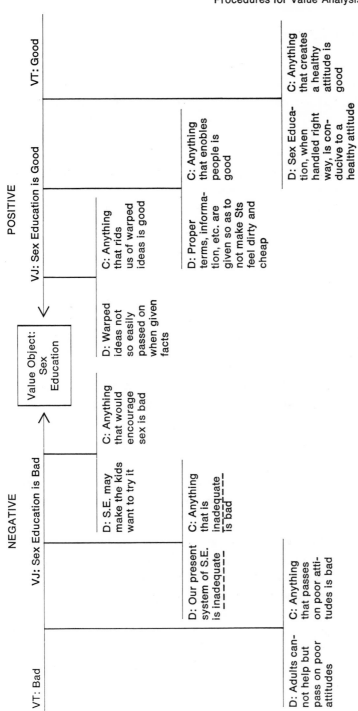

Figure 9. **Use of Extended Value Model by Student on Sex Education**

Extended Procedure

We turn now to the teaching procedure with which we have had the most success and the most experience. We will call this the *Extended Procedure*. Since it was developed originally to make the Extended Value Model more specific and manageable for all the students, there are a number of close connections. There are also a number of connections to the Rudimentary Procedure, as will be pointed out in the description. The Extended Procedure will be illustrated with one student's work on the topic of sex education. For convenience, we will call the student *Jane*.

STEP 1. *Selection of Topic.* The first step of the Extended Procedure is exactly the same as the first step of the Rudimentary Procedure. For example, the student (Jane) whose work we are using to illustrate the procedure was from a class of high school seniors of average intelligence, studying social problems of both local, regional, and national interest. And as it turned out, the scope of the topic, Sex Education, appeared to be about right. It was broad enough for the more creative advanced students, yet narrow enough for the slower ones. Furthermore, the topic was not only of international and national interest but of both regional and local interest.

STEP 2. *Provision of Adequate Materials.* The second step is exactly the same as its counterpart in Rudimentary Procedure.

STEP 3. *Provision of Proper Atmosphere.* The third step is also the same as its counterpart in the Rudimentary Procedure, with the following addition. If possible, the topic should be assigned on Friday. This allows the students the weekend to search for materials outside the school facilities. Furthermore, it gives them the opportunity to study with friends from other classes. In other words, the students should be encouraged to seek outside materials, assistance, and experiences.

STEP 4. *Listing and Ranking Positive and Negative Statements.* The student lists positive and negative statements[7] about the topic in order of their importance to the student.[8] It should be accomplished over the weekend and handed in at the end of the class period on Monday. Figure 10 (pp. 92-93) contains Jane's first folder, with positive and negative statements on Sex Education. After each statement, Jane has indicated in which Domain(s) (these are essentially the same as "concerns" in Chapter 2) she thinks the statement should be classified.

STEP 5. *Preparation of Evidence Cards.* The student prepares evidence cards by transferring each of the ranked positive and negative statements from Step 4 to 3 x 5 cards according to the format for the evidence card presented in Chapter 2.[9] This phase takes Monday's class period and evening. Preferably, it should be handed in at the end of Tuesday's class.

Figure 11 (pp. 94-95) contains Jane's second folder, with the positive and negative evidence cards.

STEP 6. *Analyzing Positive and Negative Evidence Cards.* The teacher can provide much guidance to the student on the basis of what is in Chapters 1 and 2. Thus, it is difficult to be very specific about this step. One point, however, is that each student will be personally interviewed several times during the course of the Extended Procedure. Therefore, starting with this step, the teacher should take careful notes on the students' folders to prepare beneficial questions that can be directed to the students' most critical needs in the personal interviews. For example, suppose the student's basic need is for applicable information. If it is a genuine need, it can be easily and quickly remedied by asking a student with an abundance of information to share his sources with the student who has little or no information. However, assuming that the student knows how and where to find his own information, if the problem persists, the teacher should look more closely for the real problem — laziness, lack of interest, etc.

STEP 7. *Class Discussion of the Evidence Cards.* The class discussion of the Evidence Cards preferably takes place during Tuesday's class period. It begins by having the students pass in all of their number one positive cards. These are then enlarged by an opaque projector or some similar aid so that all the students can read them. Then one by one the cards are discussed with respect to such matters as reliable sources of information, accuracy of the facts, appropriateness of the criteria, etc. Next, the number two positive cards are handed in and discussed. This is continued until the teacher and class decide to turn to the negative cards. The same routine is used for the negative cards. However, duplicates are eliminated to save time. One important feature of this step is that the cards are not signed, so the students can remain anonymous if they wish to. Furthermore, it gives the students the opportunity to see their own work (" in lights," so to speak) and they can see how others react to their thinking. In fact, many students confessed that they often asked questions about their own cards not only to get responses but answers to difficulties they had encountered.

STEP 8. *Listing and Ranking of Causes.* The student lists causes for each negative statement and ranks them. Thus, the student takes the first negative statement or Evidence Card and finds as many causes for it as he can. For example, if the topic is Air Pollution and the statement is that 80,000,000 tons of pollutants are put in the air each year, the student might list such causes as airplanes, cars, industry, and burning garbage. The student then takes the second negative statement or card and finds causes for it. This is continued until the teacher and students decide to move on. Typically the students deal with only one or two statements for which they find causes. Next the student ranks the causes for each statement or card in their order of importance. In the example of air pollution the student might rank the causes in the order: cars, industry, burning garbage, and airplanes. Finally, the student lists positive and negative statements for each cause.

This step should be completed and handed in at the end of Wednesday's class period. The significance of this step is as follows. (1) Each student can work according to his ability. For example, a slower student may only have time to work on one or two positive and negative aspects, whereas a faster student may have enough time to complete a dozen or more. Quantity, as a basis for grading, is only compared against the individual's capacity, not his fellow-classmates. (2) This phase allows the student the opportunity to discover clues or causes as to why the statements he selected are negative.

Figure 12 (pp. 96-97) contains Jane's third folder with the list of causes for her first negative statement, the causes already ranked, and positive and negative statements about each cause.

STEP 9. *Personal Interviews*. After a teacher has been through the Extended Procedure several times, he will more than likely start personal interviews during Monday's class period. However, until that time, he will start interviewing during Wednesday's class. They will continue through Thursday, Friday, and then Monday, Tuesday, Thursday, and Friday of the following week. The basic functions of the personal interview are giving information and asking questions. The first function deals mainly with suggesting additional sources of information as well as techniques of finding, recording, and organizing information without wasting valuable time and energy. The second function, asking questions, deals more with probing and prying for knowledge. In other words, the teacher should ask questions that cause the students to ponder, muse, and wonder.

The only danger here is one of indoctrination. *The teacher must be extremely careful not to impose his biases upon his students.* There is ample information available on interviewing techniques, which will help a teacher overcome this problem. Chadwick (1969) has developed an interviewing procedure which has been shown to reduce the imposition of interviewer bias and to increase the likelihood of getting honest reaction from the person being interviewed. This procedure is contained in Appendix I of this yearbook. (See pages 168-176.)

Finally, unless the teacher has very small classes, he will have only enough time for these interviews to last about five or six minutes apiece. If additional time is required, it should be scheduled for before or after school or saved for the next interview. However, as it usually works out, about a fourth of the students will use much less time than that allotted, whereas another fourth of the students could use all of the time you have. The rest average about right. Just remember, you only have a few minutes. Use them wisely and don't try to accomplish more than one or two things during that period of time.

STEP 10. *Listing and Ranking of Possible Solutions.* The student lists and ranks possible solutions for as many causes as time will allow. He also lists positive and negative aspects for each possible solution. This phase should be completed and handed in at the end of Thursday's class period. This step is similar to other steps, e.g., the eighth step, Listing and Ranking of Causes, in that it allows each student to work at his own rate of speed. It also offers him the chance to solve the problems that he faces in this and any other topic.

Figure 13 (pp. 98-103) contains Jane's fourth folder, with her possible solutions for each cause listed in order of importance to her. Then for each cause, Jane has listed positive and negative statements for each possible solution.

STEP 11. *Preparation of Positive and Negative Evidence Cards for Solutions.* The student now prepares Evidence Cards for his proposed solutions. The basic procedure here is the same as that for step five, Preparation of Evidence Cards. The students transfer the ranked positive and negative statements to 3 x 5 cards and write a criterion to go with each statement. Again, each Evidence Card corresponds to a support element in the Extended Value Model. Thus, a value judgment that some solution is good will be supported by a number of Evidence Cards each with a Description and a Criterion. This phase should be ready to hand in at the end of Friday's class.

Figure 14 (pp. 104-105) contains Jane's fifth folder, with some Evidence Cards for solutions. Due to lack of time, she had few Evidence Cards on her solutions.

STEP 12. *Group Discussions of Evidence Cards for Possible Solutions.* The students are allowed to group themselves into any number of groups for the purpose of discussing any and all possible solutions that they or their fellow students might have come up with. The purpose of this step is to stimulate free discussion, which will test and hopefully refine the proposed solutions. Appropriate points from Chapters 1 and 2 can be raised by both the teacher and the students. Furthermore, many questions will be raised that cannot be answered satisfactorily. They, in turn, will be put to use in the following phase. This phase takes place during both Monday and Tuesday class periods.

STEP 13. *Question-Answer Period with Guest Expert.* In the question and answer period, a guest expert answers students' questions as simply and quickly as possible. If any of the students feel that the guest expert has strayed from the topic, they have the right to interrupt him and ask if the majority of the class is ready to move on to another question. This phase takes place during Wednesday's class period.

STEP 14. *Observations and Recommendations.* Finally, the students prepare observations and recommendations. This is essentially the same as the last step in the Rudimentary Procedure. The observations the student found to be most significant are listed and then his recommendations.

Figure 15 (pp. 106-108) contains Jane's sixth and final folder, with her observations and recommendations on Sex Education as a result of going through the whole Extended Procedure.

(*For "Summary of Folders in Their Appropriate Steps in the Extended Procedure, see page 109*)

**Figure 10a. Jane's Folder #1,
Left Side,* with Positive Statements**

	POSITIVE	RANKING
1.	There are many varied approaches that may be suited to each individual. Education.	9
2.	It educates people instead of indoctrinating them to one certain view toward sex. Education.	7
3.	It is less likely that warped attitudes and illogical ideas will be passed on to the next generation. Viscious cycle.	1
4.	It gives all of the different views of sex that a student would not receive at home. Public understanding (psychology).	6
5.	It will educate and inform people without making them feel dirty. Proper terms are put to use with proper information. Education.	2
6.	It is ignorance that causes sexual misadventure. When a person has had their curiosity satisfied in a healthy way, they are less likely to turn to pre-marital and/or extra-marital affairs to find out about sex. Health, morals, education.	5
7.	We learn to respect the rights and views of others on sex. Public relations.	4
8.	When the right information is given in an objective manner at the right time, it is conductive to a healthy attitude toward sex. Education, public, attitudes.	3
9.	Students desire to get this information without going "to the gutter" and risking misinformation. Public, moral.	8
10.	Only small minorities oppose sex education. Public.	10

* We allowed students to select their own side for Positive and Negative statements. If our convention in this chapter is followed Positive Statements would go on the right side and Negative Statements on the left side.

**Figure 10b. Jane's Folder #1,
Right Side, with Negative Statements**

	NEGATIVE	RANKING

NEGATIVE   RANKING

1. Parents often fail to educate their youngsters in a healthy, meaningful way. Health Education.   *1*

2. There are many extreme approaches to the sex problem. Moral.   *6*

3. Adults cannot help but pass on their own illogical, guilt-ridden attitudes. Public Education, Viscious cycle.   *4*

4. The present program of sex education is very inadequate. Education.   *3*

5. Sex education might make the kids want to try it. Moral, religion.   *2*

6. Sex is evil and therefore should be avoided at all costs. Moral, religion.   *9*

7. What they don't know won't hurt them. Fear.   *8*

8. No one really wants the embarrassment and responsibility in teaching sex education. Education, politics.   *7*

9. The attempts at sex education are unorganized and they don't know what one another are doing. Public.   *5*

Figure 11a. Jane's Second Folder,
Left Side, with Positive Evidence Cards

Domain: Vicious Cycle

Criterion: Anything that rids us of warped ideas is good.

Statement: Warped ideas are not so easily passed on when students are taught sex by someone who gives them facts.

Domain: Public, Moral

Criterion: Anything that improves people through education is good.

Statement: Students are educated in a meaningful manner.

Domain: Education

Criterion: Anything that enobles people is good.

Statement: Proper terms, proper information, and proper instructions given in such a way as to not make the students feel dirty and cheap.

Domain: Health, morals, education

Criterion: Anything that prevents pre-marital or extra-marital affairs is good.

Statement: Curiosity is satisfied so people are less likely to try it.

Domain: Education, public, attitudes

Criterion: Anything that creates a healthy attitude is good.

Statement: Sex education, when handled in the right way, is conducive to a healthy attitude.

Domain: Public understanding (Psychology)

Criterion: Anything that gives different views is good.

Statement: Sex education presents all sides of sex.

Figure 11b. Jane's Second Folder,
Right Side, with Negative Evidence Cards

Domain: Health, Education

Criterion: Anything that prevents a meaningful education is bad.

Statement: Parents often fail to educate their children In a healthy, meaningful way.

Domain: Public, education, vicious cycle

Criterion: Anything that passes on poor attitudes is bad.

Statement: Adults cannot help but pass on poor attitudes.

Domain: Moral, religion

Criterion: Anything that would encourage sex is bad.

Statement: Sex education may make the kids want to try it.

Domain: Public

Criterion: Anything that is unorganized is bad.

Statement: Attempts at sex education are unorganized.

Domain: Education

Criterion: Anything that is Inadequate is bad.

Statement: Our present system of sex education is very inadequate.

Domain: Moral

Criterion: Anything that Is extreme is bad.

Statement: There are many extreme approaches to sex education.

Figure 12a. Jane's Third Folder, with List of Causes, Ranked, and Positive and Negative Statements about each Cause

Statement: People cannot help but to pass on their own misconceived ideas and poor attitudes.

List of Causes:

A. Parents

B. Society

C. Peer Groups

D. Literature (Books, magazines, movies)

E. Religion

F. Education

Cause: A. Parents

Positive	Negative
1. They pass on the way to keep the species going.	1. They often give the wrong facts or misleading ideas.
2. They give us protection from a sex-oriented world.	2. They often fail to admit that we are maturing and keep knowledge about sex from us.
3. They are usually the best judges about when we are ready to know about sex.	3. They are usually too embarrassed to tell us about sex when we are ready for it.
4. Without them, we wouldn't be here.	

Cause: B. Society

Positive	Negative
1. It's our environment.	1. Our society is so involved in sex that sex crimes are all but encouraged.
2. It's our way of life.	2. It is changeable and hypocritical.

(Continued on next page)

Figure 12b. **Jane's Third Folder, continued**

Cause: C. Peer Groups

Positive

1. They fill our need for **friend-ship** and human contact.
2. They are the ones with whom we can share our ideas and reasoning.

Negative

1. They bring the filth and dirt to us through dirty stories, books, magazines, etc.
2. Our peer group adds or starts poor attitudes about sex.

Cause: D. Literature

Positive

1. It broadens our scope of life.
2. It shows the different views of life that we would never see otherwise.

Negative

1. It helps make an overpowering drive that we cannot control.
2. It pulls people down into the gutter and makes them feel cheap.

Cause: E. Religion

Positive

1. It answers our questions about life and death.
2. It fulfills the need of having something to believe in.

Negative

1. It creates unhealthy inhibitions about sex.
2. It claims that they should be the ones to teach sex-education but they have neither the facilities nor the funds.

Cause: F. Education

Positive

1. I do not feel that education is a source of misconception and of poor attitudes.

Figure 13. Jane's Fourth Folder, with Possible Solutions for each Cause, each with Positive and Negative Statements

---

1. The most significant cause of the problem is parents.

List of possible solutions:

    A. Sex-education with schools and parents co-operating

    B. Sex-education without parents helping

    C. Sex-education in school with permission of the majority of parents

    D. Sex-education for parents

Possible Solutions

    A. Sex-education with schools and parents co-operating

Positive	Negative
1. It would give both facts and the parents' point of view.	1. Parents may still pass on warped attitudes.
2. The parents would not be feeling left out and tossed aside.	2. Parents may not co-operate.
3. Parents could "supervise" to some degree their children's education.	
4. Students have a choice of action and know the consequences of the things that they do.	
5. Warped ideas are weeded out and healthy attitudes planted.	

    B. Sex-education without parents helping

Positive	Negative
1. Warped ideas are not easily passed on.	1. Parents cannot feel that they have helped their child.
2. Students would receive the facts and be told how to use them wisely.	2. The student might very easily receive all fact and no emotion.
3. Students would know the possible consequences of certain acts.	
4. Students are taught how to perpetuate the species.	

(Continued on next page)

Figure 13. Jane's Fourth Folder, continued

C. Sex-education in school with permission of the majority of parents

Positive

Negative

1. Students would learn to perpetuate the species.

2. Students would learn to use their reproductive powers wisely.

3. The results and/or consequences of certain acts would be known.

4. Warped ideas would be forgotten.

5. Parents could give additional material, explanations, and discussions if they feel that it is needed.

6. Parents would not feel left out.

1. It would be expensive.

2. It would be difficult to find a qualified teacher.

D. Sex-education for parents

Positive

Negative

1. It would give parents a chance to learn the things that they should teach their children.

2. It would change many attitudes for the better.

3. It would be an opportunity to learn.

1. The parents would feel ashamed that they don't know enough about sex.

2. It's a little too late for people who already have kids.

2. The second most significant cause of the problem is society.

Possible Solution

There is no direct solution to a sex oriented society. A society is made up of people. When the people change, so will our society.

3. The third most significant cause of the problem are peer groups.

Possible solutions

A. Sex-education in school

B. Sex-education in church

C. Sex-education at home with schools providing material and lesson plan.

D. Sex-education with parents and schools cooperating

E. Sex-education with moral aspects taught in church, emotional aspects taught at home, and physical and hygenic aspects taught at school.

(Continued on next page)

Figure 13. Jane's Fourth Folder, continued

A. Sex-education in school

Positive

1. All students would receive equal education.

2. Students would know why sex was, what it was for, and how to use it wisely.

3. Poor attitudes about sex would be more likely to die out.

Negative

1. Students would only be taught the physical aspects of sex.

2. Students might become curious about sex and want to try it.

3. Finding a qualified teacher would be difficult.

B. Sex-education in church

Positive

1. Students would learn both the moral and the physical aspects of sex.

2. It would be up to the student to receive sex-education if he wanted it.

Negative

1. Not everyone attends church.

2. The moral aspects of sex would be over stressed.

C. Sex-education at home with schools providing materials and lesson plan.

Positive

1. Students would receive their education at home where they should learn it.

2. Not only would the students learn, but also the parents would learn. Besides that, not only sex but good attitudes.

3. Students would learn what they need to about sex.

Negative

1. It would be expensive.

2. If parents didn't have time, or were too embarrassed to present the material, the students would still be in the dark.

3. Parents may not completely understand the material and/or present it wrong.

4. The schools may not give the parents the material that they would need to answer their children's questions.

(Continued on next page)

Figure 13. Jane's Fourth Folder, continued

D. Sex-education with parents and schools co-operating.

Positive	Negative
1. Parents would be helping their children. They will be able to have some control over their kid's education.	1. Parents could pass on poor attitudes.
2. Parents will be able to inject their religious beliefs into their children.	2. If either the parents or the schools failed, the students would have a lopsided education.
3. Poor attitudes will eventually be weeded out.	

E. Sex-education with moral aspects taught in church, emotional aspects taught at home, and physical and hygenic aspects taught at school.

Positive	Negative
1. Students would learn all aspects of sex.	1. It would be very expensive.
2. Students would receive a well-rounded education.	2. Many parents and churches would be unwilling to cooperate.
3. Students would receive the information they need to become parents and on how to raise their children well.	3. Poor attitudes towards sex could still be passed on.

4. The fourth most significant causes of the problem are books, magazines, movies and other literature.

Possible Solutions

    A. Effective censorship board.
    B. Effective home control
    C. Prevent the printing of obscene material

A. Effective censorship board

Positive	Negative
1. Would help take sex out of the gutter.	1. It is difficult to define obscene.
2. It would protect our youth and older ones alike.	2. It would be hard to choose people who would make fair decisions.
3. It would upgrade our literature.	

(Continued on next page)

Figure 13. Jane's Fourth Folder, continued

B. Effective home control

Positive   Negative

1. Children usually respect thier   1. The minute they say don't, they
   parent's orders when they are   do it.
   ordered to do something. Ex-   2. We've tried it and it's failed.
   ample: To leave dirty literature
   alone.

C. Prevent the printing of obscene literature

Positive   Negative

1. It's a good way of protecting   1. It is impossible to define what
   our youth and older folks too.   is obscene and what is not.

2. It would eliminate the need for   2. Sex is a main selling point in
   a censorship board.   most movies and literature
                                          today.
3. It would be easier for parents
   to censor what their children
   read.

4. It would upgrade the type of
   literature that is written.

5. The fifth most significant cause of the problem is religion.

Possible Solution

A. Call a meeting of the heads of churches and ask them not to
   make sex dirty

Positive   Negative

1. If clergymen were made to un-   1. It would be difficult to get
   derstand that sex is not dirty if   everyone to work together.
   used right, they might help the   2. If the clergyman did not agree,
   cause of sex education.   they could start really over-
                                          emphasizing the "sinful act."

I feel that we will have to replace the present adults with someone
who has a better attitude towards sex. This will hopefully be the
upcoming generation who has received sex education.

(Concluded on next page)

Figure 13. **Jane's Fourth Folder, concluded**

6. The sixth most significant cause of the problem is education.

Possible Solution

I do not feel that education was ever a source of poor attitudes towards sex. But the sex education that I would advocate would be basically:

1. Taught by a qualified teacher.

2. In primary grades
   a. Develops wholesome attitude
   b. Use proper terminology
   c. Help them understand sex differences
   d. Use frankness
   e. Discourage masturbation
   f. Give answers
   g. Help child understand his place in the family

3. Intermediate grades
   a. Learn the reproduction of plants and animals
   b. Help them to understand changes
   c. To develop a nature attitude toward sex
   d. To respect social customs, and family loyalties
   e. Respect miracle of life

4. Adolescent
   a. Scientific background
   b. Establish respect for social standards
   c. Develop family relations
   d. Encourage frankness

5. Teach not only physical aspects, but also the emotional and moral aspects.

6. Allow parents to preview all material that will be presented to the class.

7. Separate the class by sex for the most intimate details.

Figure 14a. Jane's Fifth Folder, Left Side, with
Evidence Cards for Positive Statements about Solutions

Domain: Attitudes Public

Criterion: Anything that creates healthy attitudes is good.

Statement: Warped ideas are weeded out and replaced by healthy ones.

Domain: Ideology Public

Criterion: Anything that gives a choice of action with knowledge of consequences is good.

Statement: Students have a choice of action and knowledge of the consequences.

Domain: Public Attitudes

Criterion: Anything that allows parents to supervise their children is good.

Statement: Parents would be supervising their children's education.

Domain: Public Attitudes

Criterion: Anything that gives facts and allows expression of ideas on their use is good.

Statement: With parents and schools cooperating, facts and opinions are put out in the open.

Domain: Public Relations

Criterion: Anything that prevents hurt feelings is good.

Statement: Parents are included in the sex education program.

**Figure 14b. Jane's Fifth Folder, Right Side, with
Evidence Cards for Negative Statements about Solutions**

Domain: Public Education

Criterion: Anything that permits dissention is bad.

Statement: Parents may refuse to cooperate, resulting in a partial
education.

Domain: Attitudes Public

Criterion: Anything that allows warped attitudes is bad.

Statement: Parents may still pass on warped attitudes.

Figure 15a. Jane's Final (Sixth) Folder, Left Side, with Observations on Sex Education

OBSERVATIONS

1. People's attitudes toward sex education are a result of the period of time in which they grew up, the attitudes of thier parents, and the extent of involvement of religion in sex.

2. People who do not understand the sex education program tend to be opposed to it. They usually believe that it will only teach their children "dirty words." They may also oppose it because they don't want to feel inferior to their children in this area of knowledge. They fear that sex education might put "bad" notions into their heads.

3. People are interested about sex education, but they are either too embarrassed to talk about it or they are afraid of it. They are afraid that they will be considered dirty if they attend a sex education course. Also, they are often unwilling to admit that they don't know much about sex (especially if they are married and have a family).

4. It is a minority of people who oppose sex education. Most people are either indifferent to it, mildly in favor of it, or fanatically in favor of it.

5. We lack the trained personnel to put an effective, nation-wide program into effect.

6. "Attitudes" seems to be the key word. If we can change fearful, misconceived attitudes toward sex into healthy ones, we will have ninety percent of the problem (that is, fear and distrust of sex education) worked out.

7. We are presently at a point in a vicious cycle, that enables us to break it if we act in time. If we institute an effective sex education program within the next three years, we will not sink into a time when sex is taught with fear, "non-facts," and misconceived attitudes. People will learn to understand their sexual urges, how to control them and how to use them in a constructive way.

8. If we are going to use sex education, we must put into effect a well-organized, factual program. A poor sex education program would be worse than none at all.

Figure 15b. **Jane's Final (Sixth) Folder,**
Right Side, with Recommendations on Sex Education

RECOMMENDATIONS

I. Teachers should have a regular training program in sex education similar to the training program for English teachers, and History teachers.

II. We should set up a program in which the following are taught:

   a. The physical aspects. What happens during puberty? Intercourse? Pregnancy? Birth?

   b. The moral aspects. What do different religions feel is proper and acceptable before and after marriage? What is considered right and what is considered wrong?

   c. The psychological aspects. How do sexual urges cause problems when stifled and repressed? How do you control your sexual urges?

   d. The emotional aspects. How do we react emotionally to the different acts of sex and their results?

III. The graded steps of teaching sex as I feel they should be are:

   a. Primary grades:

     1. Develop a wholesome attitude towards sex.
     2. Use proper terminology when talking about the body.
     3. Create the understanding that there are differences between girls and boys.
     4. Discuss their problems of growing up and living in a sex-oriented world.
     5. Discourage unnecessary handling of certain parts of the body.
     6. Give correct and understandable answers to any questions on reproduction.
     7. Help each child to be a good family member — with loyalty, love and appreciation of his family.
     8. Give parents the assignment to witness with their child, the birth of kittens, puppies, or some such animal.

   b. Intermediate grades:

     1. Stress wholesome attitudes toward sex.
     2. Give students an understanding of the scientific vocabulary for discussion of natural processes.
     3. Help students understand the changes that are/or will take place in their bodies.
     4. Develop a mature attitude towards sex.

(Concluded on next page)

Figure 15b. Jane's Final Folder, concluded

5. Help boys and girls understand growth and how it is linked with heredity and physiology.

6. Develop respect for social customs.

7. Respect for life.

8. Deepen family loyalties.

c. Junior High

1. Continue to develop a wholesome and mature attitude toward sex.

2. Give students a scientific background and vocabulary to enable them to discuss sex with dignity and frankness.

3. Establish respect for social standards.

4. Help students understand why good behavior is important.

5. Develop good family relations.

6. Encourage students to talk freely about their problems and help them find the answers to them.

7. Teach them about growth, reproduction, growth and birth of a baby, heredity, boy-girl relations, venereal diseases, family relations, and the responsibilities of growing up.

d. Senior High

1. Give the students knowledge and appreciation of the family.

2. Give students the information to understand sexual urges, relation to life and the family, understanding the power of the sex drive, control of the sex urge by will power, and separating sex desire from love.

3. Help youth acquire ideals, standards, and attitudes that will help him to choose a mate and raise a family.

4. Teach students about the family, adolescence, selecting a mate, marriage preparation, the process of reproduction, promiscuity, population explosion, and ideal of life.

5. Talk to the students on an adult level, use honesty, give information and be frank.

Summary of Folders in Their Appropriate Steps in the Extended Procedure. The chart in Figure 16 should be helpful to the reader in summarizing where in the Extended Procedure each folder goes.

Figure 16. **Summary of Folders by Steps in Extended Procedure**

Folder		Step in Procedure	Figure
1	4	Listing Positive and Negative Statements	10
2	5	Positive and Negative Evidence Cards	11
3	8	Listing and Ranking of Causes	12
4	10	Listing and Ranking of Possible Solutions	13
5	11	Positive and Negative Evidence Cards for Solutions	14
6	14	Observations and Recommendations	15

Concluding Comments. The above fourteen steps make up the Extended Procedure as developed and used to this point. However, there are several variations and additions that have not been mentioned due to the fact that the writers have not had sufficient time or resources available to explore their potential. Furthermore, the majority of the Social Studies teachers that we have worked with felt that since we had already presented much new material we would do the yearbook reader a disservice by explaining all of these extra ramifications in detail.

Flexibility, Individualization, and Personalization of the Extended Procedure

As we have indicated by our description of the Extended Procedure, it has several desirable characteristics. Three of the more important ones are flexibility, individualization, and personalization.

The chart in Figure 17 describes the Extended Procedure with respect to these three characteristics. For each step, except the last, there is a Personal Interview. The columns labeled T-centered, Group-centered, and St-centered indicate the main sources of variation possible for each step, i.e., whether it is primarily teacher-centered, primarily group-

Figure 17. Flexibility, Individualization, and Personalization of Extended Procedure

Step in Procedure	T-Cen-tered	Gp-Cen-tered	St-Cen-tered	Explanatory Comment
1. Selection of Topic	1	3	6	Several groups or students could be working on separate topics.
1a. Personal Interview	1		9	Finding out St's interest
2. Provision of Adequate materials	3	2	5	Teacher fills in gaps
2a. Personal Interview	3		7	T will have broader base as a result of all PIs
3. Provision of Proper Atmosphere	3	4	3	Total class commitment
3a. Personal Interview	7		3	Dealing with discipline problems
4. Listing and Ranking Positive and Negative Statements	1	2	7	Usually personal, but others can help
4a. Personal Interview	2		8	T fills in gaps
5. Preparation of Evidence Cards	1	2	7	Mostly personal effort
5a. Personal Interview (See step 6)	2		8	Checks logical consistencies
6. See 5a				
7. Class Discussion of the Evidence Cards	1	7	2	Group discussion of individual cards
7a. Personal Interview	1		9	Get at feelings about discrepancies with group
8. Listing and Ranking of Causes	1	4	5	St interested in variety of possibilities
8a. Personal Interview	3		7	T fills in gaps
9. Personal Interviews — already covered				
10. Listing and Ranking of Possible Solutions	1	3	6	St gets more from group and sources than in Step 4
10a. Personal Interview	2		8	T interested in filling gaps and getting at feelings
11. Preparation of Positive and Negative Evidence Cards for Solutions	1	2	7	Mostly personal effort
11a. Personal Interview	1		9	Mostly getting at feelings
12. Group Discussions of Evidence Cards for Possible Solutions	0	7	3	Group discussion of individual cards
12a. Personal Interview	1		9	Getting at feelings
13. Question and Answer Period with Guest Expert	0	6	4	St-group interactions testing St's hypotheses with expert
13a. Personal Interview	1		9	Getting at feelings
14. Observations and Recommendations	0	1	9	Very personal

centered, or primarily student-centered. The numbers in the table express our judgment as to the "ideal" involvement of the teacher, the group, and the student: for each step, ten points are divided up among the teacher, group, and student to indicate their ideal proportion of involvement. The explanatory comment indicates briefly the most salient points about the step, such as its main purpose or content, especially for the "ideal" way the step would be conducted.

Flexibility. Although we indicate an "ideal" involvement for each step, the amount of variation possible, i.e., whether teacher-centered, group-centered, or student-centered, indicates the extent to which the Extended Procedure is flexible. The teacher can adapt each step to his own style, characteristics of the students, topic selected, materials available, and the like.

Individualization. The Extended Procedure allows each student to achieve some degree of success according to his ability, allows him to select his own topic so that the emphasis is upon the student's own ability to produce results. The procedure allows the student to select his own topic, to proceed at his own pace, etc. The ways this individualization can be achieved are illustrated by the following three steps. STEP 1: *Selection of topic.* The student may select as a value object something as small in scope as a decision on a typewriter he is about to buy or as large in scope as "problems of the cities." STEP 2: *Provision of source materials.* The only encroachment upon independence here is the fact that the teacher is allowed to suggest additional source material to the student for a variety of reasons; otherwise, the selection of materials is totally student-centered. STEP 3: *Class discussions of evidence cards.* Showing the evidence cards on an opaque projector with each card anonymous gives the opportunity for each student to be viewed in a completely individual way.

Personalization. The pervasive use of the personal interview by itself contributes neatly to personalization. Additional ways are the group discussions, video playbacks of the group discussions, video playbacks of personal interviews, testing of value principles, and community involvement.

Formulating the Criterion

We have found it helpful to have the student formulate a Criterion using the chart in Figure 18. After getting a Statement which contains a Characteristic of the VO, and selecting

Figure 18. Chart for Formulating a Criterion

	VO	Characteristic	VT
Value Judgment	air pollution		undesirable
Description	air pollution	produces emphysema	
Criterion	any condition*	produces emphysema	undesirable

*Comparison Class

some appropriate VT[10] which is applied to the VO, the student has two of the three parts of the Criterion. The third part is the Comparison Class. This class is more general than the VO and includes the VO as a member. All the members of the Comparison Class are what the VO is compared against in deciding whether the VT should be applied to it because of the Characteristic. The example in Figure 18 is from Figure 5. "Air pollution" is the VO, "undesirable" is the VT, "produces emphysema" is the Characteristic, and "any condition" is the Comparison Class, i.e., "air pollution" is a member of the more general class of "conditions." The student can select any one of a variety of appropriate Comparison Classes.

Progressing from the Rudimentary Procedure to the Extended Procedure in Class Discussion Form

Although we have not explored extensively the class discussion form of the Extended Model, it seems to hold some promise. The progression will be described for use with the entire class. However, it can be used with single students or small groups.

1. *Start with Positive-Negative Chart.* The first step is to start with the chart used in the Rudimentary Procedure, listing positive and negative statements about the topic (VO). Each student fills out a chart as the discussion proceeds.

2. *Adding Value Terms.* The second step is to add a VT to each statement, both positive and negative statements, entering this VT in the column next to the statement. Figure 19 illustrates how this is done. The teacher can ask for volunteers, and typically there will be a number of different VTs for each

Figure 19. Adding VTs to Chart in Rudimentary Procedure

statement. The students might even get into a heated discussion about which is the most appropriate VT for a statement. In our experience, we told the students that they could each use whatever VT they felt was most relevant or appropriate.

Note that at this point, the chart provides information for both a value judgment (the VT applied to the VO) and the description (D) that goes with it to help support the value judgment. All that is lacking is the Criterion. However, it is a good idea to have the students get some experience using the chart in Figure 19 on a number of VOs before moving on to the next step. Also, the students should have experience formulating Criteria before moving on. If the teacher wishes, the class can also rank the statements.

3. *Adding the Criteria.* The third step is adding the Criteria. Each Statement and its corresponding VT will have a Criterion formulated for it. In doing this the teacher and students will use material from Chapters 1 and 2 and the Criterion-formulating chart in Figure 18 from the previous section. Since the Criterion has three parts, and two of them are already present (the Characteristic and the VT), all the student has to do is add the Comparison Class. The full Criterion is then written in the column next to the VT.[11] Figure 20 illustrates how this is done.

After considerable experience with this step the student might try writing a complex value principle for his chart (see Chapter 1).

Figure 20. Adding Criteria

VO:_____

Negative				Positive	
Criterion	VT	Statement	Statement	VT	Criterion

Figure 21 presents an example of the use of the chart in Figure 20 in a sixth-grade class which discussed Communism.

Experiences with the Procedures

Our experiences with the procedures described in this chapter have been predominantly positive, both with the workshop for teachers that we conducted and the students with whom we have worked.

I. TEACHER REACTIONS

We conducted a three-quarter workshop for about 15 teachers representing grades from early elementary to secondary level and a variety of subject areas, including, of course, Social Studies. We focused on the Rudimentary and Extended Procedures, ignoring the pictorial models. Some of the teachers were rather successful in adapting the procedures to subject areas other than Social Studies, and other teachers in adapting the procedures to the elementary grades. Both during the workshop and since the completion of the workshop a number of the teachers spontaneously expressed enthusiasm for and even excitement with the procedures. Although such unsolicited comments and reactions are difficult to interpret, they are encouraging and do suggest both the kinds of phenomena and objective measures to explore further.

One kind of more objective measure we used to assess the teachers' reaction was the Semantic Differential (Osgood, Suci, and Tannenbaum, 1957). At the end of the workshop, we administered an eleven-scale Semantic Differential to eight teachers. The Semantic Differential was constructed so that only one topic was rated: "Model." (This was the general term we used at that time to denote our procedures.) The Evalu-

NEGATIVE

Criterion	VT	Statement
Any government which doesn't allow freedom of speech is terrible.	Terrible	Doesn't allow freedom of speech.
Any government which doesn't like religion is terrible.	Terrible	Doesn't like religion.
Any government in which people hand in money and no property is unfair.	Unfair	People hand money in and no property.
Any government which owns all the property is unjust.	Unjust	Government owns all property.
Any government which has no freedom of press is uneducational.	Uneducational	No freedom of press.
Any government which doesn't allow criticism of the government is awful.	Awful	Not allowed to criticize government.
Any government which has no freedom of gathering is unfair.	Unfair	No freedom of gathering.
Any government which has no freedom from fear is cruel.	Cruel	No freedom from fear.
Any government which limits picture taking is unreasonable.	Unreasonable	Limited picture taking.
Any government which has freedom to vote but only for those the party wants is unjust.	Unjust	Have freedom to vote but it's for those the party wants.

POSITIVE

Statement	VT	Criterion
Equal standard of living.	Good, Fair	Any government which has equal standard of living is good (fair).
Businessmen work for government & therefore can't fail.	Fair, Just	Any government in which businessmen work for gov't & therefore can't fail is fair (just).
Only 5% of people in USSR belong to the party.	Reasonable	Any gov't in which only 5% of the people belong to the party is reasonable.
They don't have to think of controversial issues.	Uneducational	Any gov't in which people don't have to think of controversial issues is uneducational.

Figure 21. Use of the Chart on the VO Communism in a Sixth-Grade Class Discussion

ation, Potency, and Activity dimensions were represented by standard seven-point scales. The other scales were more specialized scales such as useful-useless, relevant-irrelevant, successful-unsuccessful, and predictable-unpredictable. The eight teachers rated the Model as quite good, desirable, and useful; fairly relevant, successful, and safe; and slightly strong and unpredictable.

II. STUDENT REACTIONS

As with the teachers, one of the kinds of assessments of interest is spontaneous and unsolicited comments and reactions to the models and procedures. The following observations all refer to students in the classes within which the Extended Procedure was developed.

Two kinds of "cognitive" outcomes seem to stand out. (1) The procedure facilitates individualization; each student is able to achieve some degree of success according to his ability. The emphasis is not upon quantity *per se* but upon the individual's *ability* to produce quantity. (2) Teacher judgments and interviews with students indicate that the procedure requires fewer assignments and less severe grading practices, yet results in greater volume of work, depth of understanding, and participation in group discussions.

Two kinds of "affective" outcomes seem to stand out. (1) Level of motivation to work with the procedure is high. This may be because each student is doing something individually on the topic, and thus can see more clearly than with other teaching approaches the bearing of the topic on his life. (2) The procedure has generated much student enthusiasm — even excitement — on such problems as environmental pollution, crime, civil rights, Vietnam war, and sex education. About twenty students actually *requested* a summer course dealing with the Extended Procedure; the students developed a program for sex education to submit for consideration by the Utah Education Association, Granite Education Association, and the Utah State Board of Education.

In the two-year period since developing the Extended Procedure, 40-50 students from the classes in which it was developed have called the teacher of the class (Chadwick), the calls ranging from 1 to 18 calls per student and averaging about 6 to 7 calls per student. Some students ask for materials on the model; some ask if anything has been done such as reporting our research with them; some (2 or 3) ask to see the videotapes we made of their group discussions; and some (about 12) ask for their folders back that they made (the same kind as Jane's in this chapter). Almost all the students report that the experience with the model has influenced their lives, with the extent of the influence they have felt ranging from "some influence" to "quite a lot." More specifically, they report such kinds of influence as more questioning of facts and their sources, and less satisfaction with "pat" solutions.

Some objective measures of what the students are doing during the Extended Procedure can be obtained by counting the number of things done in some of the steps. We counted the number of statements the student collected, the number of Evidence Cards written (although they were required to write six Evidence Cards each for positive and negative statements), the number of causes listed for each of the most important negative problems, and the number of possible solutions for each of the most important ranked causes. These results are presented in Table 1 for two classes, one with

Table 1. Frequency of Occurrence of Statements, Evidence Cards, Causes, and Possible Solutions for the Topics of Crime and Civil Rights

	Topic	
Step in Extended Procedure	Crime[1]	Civil Rights[2]
4. Listing Positive Statements	8.4	15.2
Listing Negative Statements	10.0	14.5
5. Preparation of Evidence Cards		
Positive	6.0	6.3
Negative	6.0	6.3
8. Listing Causes		
For First Ranked Negative Problems	3.3	5.1
For Second Ranked Negative Problems	—	0.2
10. Listing Possible Solutions		
For First Ranked Cause	2.8	5.0
For Second Ranked Cause	0.7	0.1

[1] N = 18; 10-day period
[2] N = 9; 25-day period
(summer school)

18 students who used the Extended Procedure on the value object Crime, and another class with nine students who used the Extended Procedure on the value object Civil Rights. Two points are worth noting. (1) Although the second class worked on Civil Rights more than twice as long as the first class worked on Crime, the difference between the classes in the number of statements, causes, and possible solutions does not reflect this extra time. (2) Although many negative statements are listed, essentially only one of these, the most important, is considered in listing causes and solutions. Thus, much more could be done on each value object.

Summary

There are many points about the procedures in this chapter that we would like to discuss. However, we feel that most of these points would not be particularly meaningful to the reader without having experienced them. We recommend to the reader that he go through the procedures a number of times with a number of topics and issues, e.g., starting with the Rudimentary Procedure and progressing to the Extended Procedure. On each issue he can look for relationships among the various steps and aspects of the procedures and the relationships to the material in the other chapters. In this way he will acquire his own experience, and the procedures and the background in other chapters will gradually become more meaningful to him.

(For Procedure for Personal Interviews, see Appendix, pages 168-176.)

NOTES

[1] This permits each student the opportunity to study the topic the way he wants to — individually, in any grouping, or combination of the two.

[2] Some of the brighter students, however, liked the Extended Value Model very much (in discussions of pollution problems).

[3] The value judgment, then, is the application of the value term (VT) to the value object (VO).

[4] In the language used in Chapter 1, these four elements are, respectively, the value object, evaluative term or rating term, fact or factual statement, and criterion.

[5] The following account of the Extended Value Model is adapted from Milton Meux, *A General Value Model,* Copyright, 1970. Permission to use Figures 7 and 8 in the account here is granted by the author.

[6] A support element is a description-criterion combination, represented in the diagram by a single vertical-horizontal line combination, the horizontal line here being the lower one, e.g., the one just above D_1 and C_1.

[7] The statements correspond to Description (D) in the pictorial Extended Value Model. The division into positive and negative statements corresponds to the right and left hand sides, respectively, in the pictorial model.

[8] Not only is the order of importance what the student *himself* thinks is the order, but whether each statement is positive or negative is up to the student himself. In terms of Chapter 1, a single statement has positive valence for the student if he lists it as positive, negative valence if he lists it as negative.

[9] The Evidence Card corresponds to the support element in the Extended Value Model. Thus the student can have as many Evidence Cards as he wants.

[10] The VT and Characteristic must be relevant or appropriate to each other.

[11] After considerable experience with this step, the full Criterion could be eliminated and just the Comparison Class entered in this column.

REFERENCES

Chadwick, J. C. "A Study to Develop an Interviewing Procedure for Decreasing Imposition of Viewpoints and Increasing Honest Reaction." Unpublished Ed.D. Dissertation. University of Utah, 1969.

Osgood, C. E., G. J. Suci, and P. H. Tannenbaum. *The Measurement of Meaning.* Urbana, Illinois: University of Illinois Press, 1957.

4

Resolving
Value Conflicts

MILTON MEUX

☐ Much has been written on the topic of conflict and conflict resolution, including the nature and kinds of conflict (Boulding, 1962; McNeil, 1965), the functions of social conflict (Coser, 1956), the causes of conflict (Mudd, 1966), the relation of conflict to defense mechanisms (Miller and Swanson, 1960), and kinds of conflict resolution (Mudd, 1966; Kelman and Baron, 1968). There is even a separate journal devoted to conflict resolution: *Journal of Conflict Resolution.*

In spite of all that has been written about conflict resolution, there is little that will help the teacher in resolving value conflicts. Several factors seem responsible for this deficit. First, many of the writings are of questionable relevance to resolving *value* conflicts.[1] Second, what there is that might be relevant is not in such a form that it helps the teacher *do* something specific; there are no operations or strategies suggested. Third, little research has been done specifically on conflict resolution in educational contexts. Fourth, much of the literature on conflict resolution leaves the reader with the impression that conflict-resolving activities must involve one in coercion, power struggles, imposition of biases, conformity, etc., and therefore is not rational or educationally relevant, much less appropriate.

The purpose of this chapter is to present some systematic ways of trying to achieve Objective 3, the resolving of value conflict. Although we have had little experience with the strategies and procedure we will outline here, they are based largely on the previous analyses in Chapters 1 and 2, and on the procedural principles used in Chapter 3. What we present here is sufficiently open and flexible that the teacher can add to it as he learns about conflict and ways to manage it in rational and educationally appropriate ways. Further, we emphasize here, as in previous chapters, operations the teacher and students can perform.

Our treatment has several limitations. First, the kind of value conflict for which we suggest teaching strategies and a procedure is restricted to conflict in value judgments. Thus, although we suggest ways to reduce differences in criteria and between principles, these conflicts are not the primary focus.

Consider the following examples of conflicts between the value judgments of persons A and B.

Person A	Person B
(1) The use of pesticides is inadvisable.	The use of pesticides is necessary.
(2) The supersonic transport is worthless.	The supersonic transport is undesirable.
(3) The Mona Lisa is beautiful.	The Mona Lisa is not beautiful.
(4) The internal combustion engine is outmoded.	The internal combustion engine is effective.
(5) The author's argument is not fair.	The author's argument is effective.
(6) The Crime Control Bill is reactionary.	The Crime Control Bill is necessary.
(7) The U.S. involvement in Vietnam is immoral.	The U.S. involvement in Vietnam is good.

The above examples reflect a variety of value conflicts, and still other kinds could be illustrated. While these might require strategies and procedures differing somewhat in certain details, the strategies and procedures we describe at a general level can be used for any type of value conflict, i.e., between value judgments with the same value object.

Second, we assume that if there is a conflict between value judgments, the source of the conflict must be a difference in the way one or more of the six tasks described in Chapter 2 were carried out in the formulation of the value judgments. For example, the persons in conflict may have worked with different value questions, or they may have assembled different purported facts, or they may have assessed their purported facts differently, and so on for the rest of the six tasks. In our treatment of teaching strategies, we will describe for each of the six tasks first the main kinds of differences that might arise and then suggestions to the teacher for ways of resolving these differences.

Third, for convenience we shall restrict the discussion to the case of the teacher or moderator resolving value conflict between two persons. The reader can readily extend our suggestions to resolving value conflict among more than two persons, or even among groups.

Fourth, we will ignore here such problems as causes of value conflict and the "psychological meaning" of the conflict to the persons in the conflict. We do this not because these problems are unimportant. Rather, we want to present some teaching strategies and a procedure within which these other problems can fit, and an adequate treatment of how these other problems can fit in our framework is beyond the scope of this yearbook.

Teaching Strategies for Resolving Value Conflicts

The reader will recall that the purpose of Chapter 2 was to discuss teaching strategies for value analysis, i.e., ways in which the teacher can manage the performance of the six tasks in a value analysis so as to achieve Objectives 1 and 2. The purpose of this section is parallel to that of Chapter 2 — here we discuss teaching strategies for resolving value conflicts, i.e., ways in which the teacher can manage the performance of tasks which are involved in achieving Objective 3. There are six tasks which parallel the six tasks involved in achieving Objectives 1 and 2. The six tasks for Objective 3 are as follows.

1. Reducing Differences in the Interpretation of the Value Question

2. Reducing Differences in the Purported Facts Assembled

3. Reducing Differences in the Assessed Truth of Purported Facts

4. Reducing Differences in the Relevance of Facts

5. Reducing Differences in the Tentative Value Judgments

6. Reducing Differences in Testing the Acceptability of Value Principles

The teacher thus has a dual role, seeing that the tasks are performed so as to resolve the value conflict and seeing that each student's performance still meets the standards for rational value judgments.

I. REDUCING DIFFERENCES IN THE INTERPRETATION OF THE VALUE QUESTION

One source of value conflict that is often overlooked is some difference in the interpretation of the value question for which each person has responded with a value judgment. In Chapter 2, in the discussion of the task "Identifying and Clarifying the Value Question," a number of ways in which a value question can be unclear were pointed out. These included elliptical statements, vagueness or ambiguity in the term used to refer to the value object, and uncertainty about the point of view from which the evaluation is to be made. Each of these ways in which a value question can be unclear can lead to differences in the way the value question is interpreted, and thus to conflict in the value judgments eventually decided upon. In fact, there is little hope of resolving value conflict at all without agreement on the value question. On the other hand, the value conflict could be resolved to a large extent just through removing differences in the interpretation of the value question. For each of these three sources of disagreement we will point out briefly how the teacher can help the two persons in conflict.

a. Filling out elliptical statement. Here the teacher can use such comments as:

Perhaps the first thing both of you should do is to be sure you are considering the same value question.

Both of you have stated your value questions rather tersely. Could you both expand your questions so we know just what you both mean?

b. Clarifying terms in the value question. Here the teacher can use such comments as:

One of you seems to be using the term one way and the other is using the term another way. Do you think you could settle on just one use?

Here the teacher is more direct about the outcome of the difference:

Using the term in one way, we might arrive at a negative evaluation, whereas using the term another way, we might arrive at a positive evaluation. For example if we use the term "socialized medicine" to mean that the government pays all doctors the same fee, then we might evaluate socialized medicine negatively, whereas if we use the term "socialized medicine" to mean that the government pays doctors on a schedule similar to what they now receive in private practice, we might evaluate socialized medicine positively.

If the teacher is using examples to help clarify the terms, he might use such comments as:

Let's try some examples and see if both of you agree on them.

As you can see by your examples, you two aren't using the term the same way.

c. Clarifying point of view. Here the teacher can use such comments as:

Perhaps you are each using a different point of view without realizing it.

Do you realize that you are using different points of view? This is acceptable, of course, but it is important to know that you are doing this.

It is usually recognized that if you evaluate something from two different points of view, such as the moral and economic, that you can come up with different evaluations. Do you think you are using different points of view?

You may disagree on which point of view is more important, but you should at least see that the two different points of view will probably give you different evaluations.

We pointed out in the discussion of Objectives 1 and especially 2 that there may be good reasons for occasionally postponing clarification. A similar point can be made here. Although it is very likely that there will be some difference between the two persons in how they interpret the value question, it may help the persons feel the importance of this source of conflict if they attempt to reduce other kinds of differences first.

II. REDUCING DIFFERENCES IN THE PURPORTED FACTS ASSEMBLED

Differences in the purported facts assembled can clearly be a source of value conflict, since different facts about the value object are more likely than not to lead to different value judgments. (See the discussion in Chapter 1 of Standard III concerning the consideration of a wide range of facts.) The two main kinds of differences here are in the confusion of facts assembled, especially in the number and valence of facts and in the kinds and relative importance of concerns or points of view represented.

a. Distinguishing factual from evaluative assertions. In Chapters 1 and 2 techniques for distinguishing factual and evaluative assertions were discussed. Knowing these techniques, the teacher can use them in appropriate situations with such comments as:

Are you both sure that you have all factual assertions here, and not any evaluative assertions.

Remember that if a statement has a word like "undesirable" or "effective" or "adequate" then it's not a factual assertion.

John, you have as one of your facts that the draft is necessary in a cold war, whereas Bill has as one of his facts that we have always had some form of draft in times of war. Do you both see that John's statement is an evaluative statement but Bill's is a factual one?

b. Reducing differences in the range of facts considered. As already indicated, differences in the range of facts will typically lead to different value judgments. When the teacher sees that one person is leaving out facts that the other has included, he can point this out with such comments as:

Both of you should compare your facts with those of the other person. You will each see that you are missing facts the other person has included. You might consider adding those facts.

Even more direct would be comments which pinpoint where the differences are:

John, most of your facts reflect your economic concerns, whereas Bill's facts reflect mostly his political concerns. Do both of you wish to maintain your limited concerns? What implications do you think this difference has?

Although both of you have facts reflecting your political and economic concerns, John's economic facts are mostly negative for him and his political facts are positive for him. On the other hand, Bill's economic facts are mostly positive for him and his political facts are negative for him. Perhaps both of you are ignoring some important facts in these areas of concern for you.

If the persons have used the Fact-Assembly Chart described in Chapter 2 for organizing their purported facts, this chart provides a simple way of locating their differences. It allows the two persons to check quickly any differences in the concerns represented, whether facts in common have the same valence, and whether facts are general or specific. The teacher's comments will then be directed to important differences in the charts of the two persons.

III. REDUCING DIFFERENCES IN THE
ASSESSED TRUTH OF PURPORTED FACTS

It has frequently been observed that conflict between two persons' value judgments rests heavily on one fact. When this is the source of conflict, the evidence for that fact takes on added importance, and the persons in conflict would do well to concentrate their attention on a careful assessment of this crucial fact.

In general, differences in the assessment of the truth of purported facts arise from lack of knowledge of rules of evidence, from using or accepting different standards of strictness in assessing evidence, or from differences in the weight attached to different authorities and experts. Techniques and methods for reducing these differences have been developed gradually over the centuries. These are essentially problems in scientific method and rules of evidence.

a. Lack of knowledge of rules of evidence. Here the teacher can examine or encourage the persons to examine the evidence for each important fact about which the two persons differ.[2] Examples of appropriate comments by the teacher are:

Perhaps both of you should examine your evidence for the truth of that purported fact.

There is an important rule of evidence you are ignoring, John, when you claim that to be true. Just because two things are closely related, it doesn't mean that one causes the other. For example, just because height and weight are related, it doesn't mean that one causes the other. Both are influenced by a third, a general growth factor.

b. Differences in standards of strictness. Some people have higher standards of strictness for evidence than others, and some situations call for stricter standards than others. These differences may show up, e.g., in the number of specific facts a person uses as backing or evidence for his general facts. Examples of appropriate teacher comments here are:

John and Bill, you differ greatly in how critical you are of the evidence for generalization. What effects will this have?

John, you seem to be satisfied with a general factual statement with no specific evidence to support it. Bill, on the other hand, isn't satisfied until he has two or three specific facts to provide evidence for a more general fact. How do you two think this difference would affect your value judgments?

IV. Reducing Differences in the Relevance of Facts

Much value conflict stems from the differences between persons in the relevance of a given fact, or in the relative emphasis on each of a set of facts. These differences have little or nothing to do with the assessed truth of the facts. Sometimes a purported fact may have a high degree of evidence but not be very relevant, whereas other purported facts have little evidence but are highly relevant to a value judgment.[3] However, we will assume here that the persons are working with purported facts that both agree are assessed as true. Two kinds of differences in relevance are encountered.

a. Relevance vs. irrelevance of a fact. In this difference one person considers a given fact to be relevant, whereas the other person considers it to be irrelevant. For example, in a discussion of the use of DDT, the given fact might be that DDT requires greatly increasing doses to kill the insects on which it is used. John may consider this relevant and Bill may consider it irrelevant. If both persons formulate a criterion it is easier to identify the source of the difference. John's criterion might be "Any pesticide which requires greatly increasing doses to kill the insects on which it is used is dangerous." Bill, after considering this criterion, may decide that it carries no weight with him. This may be because he is concerned primarily with using a cheap insecticide with a stable market, or because there are for him no practical alternatives. John, in turn, may reflect further on why the criterion carries weight with him and find that he is concerned with the long-run problems of ecology and starting large-scale research programs to replace any dangerous pesticides.

Typically, these differences between persons in relevance of a fact depend in turn upon differences between persons in the importance of various concerns. For example, to a person who is deeply concerned about health and little about economics, the fact that air pollution produces emphysema is of great relevance. On the other hand, this fact is less relevant to a person who is less concerned about health than he is about short-term economic disturbances which could result from attempts to curb air pollution through installing expensive controls.

The teacher's comments when encountering this kind of difference would presumably point out the difference, ask each of the persons to formulate his criterion, and try to find the difference in concerns which is influencing the difference in the weight attached to the criterion:

> John, you are treating that fact as highly relevant to your value judgment. But Bill, for you the fact seems to be irrelevant. Can you two tell why it is you view the relevance of the same fact so differently?

> John, you consider that fact to be relevant, whereas Bill doesn't. Could you each formulate your criterion and see how much it means to you, how much weight it carries with you?

> Now that you have each formulated a criterion for that fact, why do you think you differ here?

Or the teacher might be more direct in suggesting that the two persons have different concerns in the issue:

> Do you think you might have different concerns that are resulting in your attaching different weights to your criteria?

> John and Bill, do you think that the main reason you differ so much in the relevance you attribute to that fact might be that you have very different concerns? Suppose you try to clarify what your concerns are and how important each concern is.

The teacher might also ask the students to focus on the implications of their differences:

> John and Bill, what implications do you think your differences might have? Bill, since you consider that fact about

DDT to be irrelevant, what would that imply for you with respect to actions you might take or recommend, plans you might adopt or recommend, etc.?

Such directing of attention to the differing emphasis on concerns may lead to a reduction in differences, since each person may unknowingly be giving more emphasis to his most important concern than he would after explicit reflection on the matter. If each person reflects on the implications of his emphasis with respect to actions taken or plans formulated, the more even balance of concerns that comes about not only helps reduce differences between the persons but is more to each person's own satisfaction.

b. Positive valence vs. negative valence of a fact relevant to both persons. A given fact may have positive valence for one person and negative valence of a fact relevant to both persons. A given fact may have positive valence for one person and negative valence for the other person. For example, suppose the given fact is that DDT decomposes slowly in the environment. For John this has negative valence and for Bill this has positive valence. John's criterion might be "Any pesticide which decomposes slowly in the environment is dangerous," whereas Bill's criterion is "Any pesticide which decomposes slowly in the environment is (more) effective." Again it turns out that the concerns of John and Bill are different: John is concerned with the long-lasting danger to the whole ecology, whereas Bill is concerned with the long-lasting killing power of DDT, which in turn results in practical savings in time, effort, and even increased safety brought about by fewer sprayings.

Teacher comments are similar to those made by the teacher when the kind of difference in relevance is relevance vs. irrelevance of a fact. (See IV.a. above.)

V. Reducing Differences in Tentative Value Judgments

Another source of conflict might be in coming to a tentative value judgment too quickly or making it too general. The teacher might facilitate reducing differences here in three ways.

a. The teacher can suggest that a general value judgment can be split into two or more specific value judgments. The teacher might comment as follows:

John and Bill, although you disagree about whether DDT is good (a general value term), you may agree that DDT is cheap and practical (both specific value terms), but still disagree on whether DDT is safe (a specific value term).

b. The subsidiary value judgments in the Fact-Assembly Chart can be examined, after which either or both persons may wish to change any of these, or rerank them. This would probably lead to a different tentative value judgment.

c. Both persons can try a variety of value judgments continually through the resolution process. This might increase flexibility in the alternative value judgments considered, and should probably start fairly early in the process.

VI. Reducing Differences in Testing the Acceptability of Value Principles

The other tasks in resolving value conflict focus on reducing differences having to do with the first three standards of rationality discussed in Chapter 1, i.e., the standards involving the truth of purported facts, the relevance of facts, and a wide range of facts. If, after performing these tasks, differences in the value judgments, and therefore the value principles of the two persons, still remain then each person's value principle is unacceptable to the other person. How can this difference in the acceptability of the value principles be reduced? How can the four tests for the acceptability of value principles be conducted so as to reduce this difference in the acceptability of the value principles?[4]

The general answer to these questions is that differences in the acceptability of the value principles are reduced by increasing the base of considerations and experiences common to the two persons in the tests of their principles.[5] In the New Cases Test, common new cases are examined. In the Subsumption Test, common higher-order principles are examined. In the Role Exchange Test, common adversely affected cases are examined. In the Universal Consequences Test, common consequences of the action are examined. To the extent that the examination of this increased common base of experience in the principle testing results in either or both of the value principles being changed, then the acceptability of each value principle to the other person is greater.[6]

1. *New Cases Test.* As indicated in Chapter 2, the New Cases Test involves proposing a new case which has the same characteristics as those in the value principle, evaluating the new case, and deciding whether the evaluation of the new case can be accepted. Thus, the persons may differ in the cases imagined and in the relative importance attached to the cases. For example, each person may come with new cases favorable to his principle but not with cases which compel him to change his principle.

The teacher can help the two persons imagine new cases, help the persons pool their own new cases, rank them in importance, and consider them in order of importance. In considering the cases, the teacher can help each person determine the extent to which the case would modify his principle, i.e., which characteristics to add, delete, or modify. One way in which each person may be of use to the other is to propose cases which are most negative for the other person's principle. These negative cases are the most important to consider when time is limited, since they have the greatest impact on the person testing his principle.

Teacher comments in the New Cases Test would be directed to such points as the following:

Have you each examined the other's new cases to see the bearing they might have on your value principle?

Those are interesting cases, but we should consider the most important ones first.

Now that you have each examined the implications of your new cases for your principles, see if your principles now have more characteristics in common.

You both have new cases which fit your value principle, but your cases all favor your principles. Let's see if we can't come up with cases for each of you that have the characteristics in your value principle but which you would evaluate differently than the class of things in your principle.

As a somewhat more extended example, consider the following situation, in which John and Bill have each formulated a value judgment on military service. John's value judgment is "Military service is vital" and Bill's is "Military service is undesirable." John's facts are that military service contributes to military preparedness and that military service is a maturing experience for a young man. Thus, his implied value principle might be "Any requirement of young people which contributes to military preparedness and is a maturing experience is vital." Bill's facts, on the other hand, are that military service detracts from development of a career and that many men who are drafted are given mundane jobs that do not contribute to our military preparedness. Thus, Bill's implied value principle might be "Any requirement of young people which detracts from the development of a career and gives them mundane jobs that are not relevant to military service is undesirable." John's new case is: "In Israel, young men serve in the military, contributing to their country's preparedness — which is vital to protect Israel against the surrounding Arab countries — and is also a maturing experience." Bill's new case is: "Some young men with potential for great careers in social science and other young men with potential for great careers in government where they could contribute much to society are put in the infantry and are killed in action."

The teacher comments on these new cases:

You each proposed a case which is favorable to your own value principle. Let's consider one that is unfavorable to your principle. John, let's take yours first. Take the case of the Nazi Youth Corps. This fits the characteristics in your principle, that the military service contribute to the military preparedness of the country and that it be a maturing experience. Would you consider serving in the Nazi Youth Corps to be vital, as your principle would imply? If not, what characteristics would you want to put in or take out of your value principle so that such a case would not be included in your principle?

2. *Subsumption Test.* As indicated in Chapter 2, the Subsumption Test involves finding a more general principle already accepted by the person, finding facts which relate this more general principle to the principle being tested, and showing that the principle being tested can be validly deduced from the more general principle and the facts. Thus the two persons may differ in the more general principles selected and in the selection of facts to connect the more general principle to the principle being tested. These differences have already been discussed under the second, third, and fourth tasks, i.e., assembling, assessing, and clarifying the relevance of facts.

Two main kinds of differences might be reduced, one in which each person has a different principle, and the other where both persons have the same principle but have different facts.

a. DIFFERENT PRINCIPLES. If the two persons have different principles, the teacher might try to determine if the difference is a real one or is a result of slightly different wording or somewhat different levels of generality. The teacher's comments might be:

Let's compare the more general principles that you accept. Are they really saying something different, or are they pretty much the same?

Perhaps you two have the same general principle, which you could determine if you examine your general principles more closely.

We can illustrate what the teacher might do here with our example above on military preparedness.

John and Bill, when we look at why you each accept the value principle you do, we find that John accepts his principle because it is vital to keep our society strong and Bill accepts his principle because it is undesirable to keep the young people in a country from developing their working capacity. Bill, if you examine your more general principle, do you think that you might be saying that if the young people in a country develop their working capacity it keeps society strong? I'm not trying to put words in your mouth, but if that seems right to you, then you both have the same more general principle, that it is important or vital to keep our society strong. Your conflict, then, is over how to keep it strong.

b. DIFFERENT FACTS. If the two persons have the same principle but different facts, the teacher might try to reduce differences by having the two persons add more purported facts so that they would have a greater set of facts in common or to assess the truth of the facts on hand. Ways of accomplishing this were discussed (p. 125-128) under the tasks "Reducing Differences in the Purported Facts Assembled" and "Reducing Differences in the Assessed Truth of Purported Facts." With respect to the example with John and Bill on military preparedness, the teacher might comment as follows:

Now that you have both agreed that your general principle involves keeping society strong, let us examine more closely the facts which connect this more general principle you both accept with your value principles that are in disagreement. John, you seem to have a fact to the effect that military preparedness keeps a society strong. Bill, you seem to have a fact to the effect that if young people can develop their careers this will keep society strong.

3. *Role Exchange Test.* As indicated in Chapter 2, the Role Exchange Test involves the person exchanging roles with someone who is most adversely affected by the action being evaluated. Perhaps the two most important differences that would arise in this test are in the roles considered and in the reactions to the action while in the role.

The basis for the judgment of who is most adversely affected may depend considerably on the person's basic concerns. The teacher's comments in this situation might be as follows:

It seems as though you two are disagreeing on whom will be most adversely affected by this action because of your basic concerns.

This kind of problem is discussed to some extent, along with the kinds of comments the teacher might make, in the section below under Role Exchange Test.

Differences in reactions to the action while in the role may be reduced by describing in more detail the adverse circumstances of the role into which the person is putting himself. An example of this technique is given in Chapter 2 where the Role Exchange Test is discussed.

4. *Universal Consequences Test.* As indicated in Chapter 2, the Universal Consequences Test involves the person asking of the action being evaluated what would happen if everyone did that. The two persons would differ here mainly in the consequences that would occur as a result of everyone doing the action being evaluated. Ways of handling these differences are discussed under the task "Assessing the Truth of Purported Facts Assembled."

Teaching Strategies for Resolving Value Conflicts: Guaranteed Minimum Yearly Income

In the first section we discussed the kinds of things a teacher can do in formulating teaching strategies for resolving value conflicts. These strategies are appropriate in either short or long resolutions of value conflicts. Since the suggestions have little context, we thought it would be helpful to present an actual conflict resolution between two persons. This resolution was on the issue of a guaranteed minimum yearly income (to be abbreviated GMYI), was between Keith and Terry, two graduate students in educational psychology, was moderated by the author, and was taped, transcribed, and edited for the purposes of clarity and coherence. Each person had read a considerable amount on the subject, had gathered a variety of facts, and brought a tentative value judgment to the discussion. Those value judgments were in conflict. A blackboard was used to record salient points, such as facts, criteria, and principles, and modifications of these as a result of the discussion. We recommend strongly the use of a blackboard to aid in keeping the discussion focused on relevant points.

1. Reducing Differences in the Interpretation of the Value Question. Keith started out with the value judgment "The Schwartz plan[7] is desirable" and Terry with the value judgment "GMYIs as stated to date are undesirable." In trying to reduce the differences in the interpretation of the value question, the moderator pointed out the importance of agreeing on a single value object:

M: Now one thing in this particular approach is that we do have to agree on the same value object. Sometimes it isn't even clear that the same term is being used in different ways, but definitely when he (Keith) says the Schwartz plan and you say the whole set of plans, that will lead to conflict right away.

T: Well, of course, by my saying that all of them are undesirable, I'm including the Schwartz plan. So the value object, the value judgment in the whole value question is included.

The moderator also pointed out that different levels of generality were involved in the value question:

M: Is the disagreement . . . Terry, are you saying that the general idea is undesirable, or even worse, or are you saying that policies that we are starting to formulate are undesirable, or is it certain plans? We have different levels of generalities here.

In attempting to decide on a common value object, a number of interesting tendencies emerged. One was to discuss the positive and negative characteristics of various value objects, i.e., other particular plans for GMYI, in the process of trying to arrive at a common value object. A second and closely related tendency was to suggest or state criteria for a sound GMYI plan. Keith felt that the Schwartz plan was the most desirable of all the specific GMYI plans now available, especially from his point of view, which was that the income level be brought up and that the economy not be jeopardized. Terry, on the other hand, held that all specific plans as stated to date were undesirable, since none of them met certain economic criteria such as not causing inflation, and that included the

Schwartz plan. Terry did say, however, that there were *some* characteristics of the specific plans that he could go along with. And Keith did point out that all the GMYI plans, even the Schwartz plan, have negative characteristics. A third tendency is to bring up facts about the initial value object.

What the persons seem to be doing during this phase is to tease out important dimensions of the value question. This is probably done as an important part of the process of selecting or deciding upon the best value object on which to focus. The best value object for each person is the one which best meets his concerns about the general problem area, in this case having enough money to live on. For example, at one point Keith said that he had picked the Schwartz plan because, on balance, its features made it for him the most desirable of all the plans. Terry, on the other hand, after the discussion had gone on for some time, said he picked the Nixon plan because it was the most realistic choice, since this plan is now being considered in Congress.

The moderator should keep track of these tendencies and efforts to arrive at an optimum selection of the value object. If it looks like it would be more fruitful to switch to another value object, he can point out what is going on and suggest a change. If a change is not in accord with what the two persons want to do, then the moderator should curtail tendencies to wander and should bring the discussion back to relevant points.

In discussing ways of improving the performance of this first task, we agreed that before starting any discussion of conflict resolution each person should already have written down or specified in some way what he considers the value question to be. This saves time by reducing discussion about what all the alternative value questions about this topic might be, and the positive and negative characteristics of each interpretation of the value question. Also, if each person specifies before the discussion what his value judgment is, and attempts to keep in mind that he is trying to see that his concerns are expressed as well as possible in some value object, then he is more likely to be focusing on his own concerns and not inadvertently selecting a value judgment which represents someone else's concern (a friend, parent, teacher, etc.). If both persons have arrived at a value judgment after going through the tasks in Chapter 2 or any of the procedures in Chapter 3, then these value judgments and all other materials can be used in the conflict resolution.

2. Reducing Differences in the Purported Facts Assembled. In order to reduce differences in the purported facts assembled, it helps to have some systematic way by which the two persons present their purported facts to each other. One convenient way is to use the Fact-Assembly Chart described in Chapter 2. Although Keith and Terry did not use every feature of the Fact-Assembly Chart, they did use a number of such features. Their facts are presented in Figure 1. In actual practice the sets of purported facts of the two persons will not be on the same page, but they can be placed next to each other to facilitate comparison.

Discussion of the differences in purported facts was interspersed throughout much of the discussion. For example, they were introduced in the identification of the value question (as already indicated), and later in clarifying the relevance of facts and in testing value principles. These purported facts were not limited to those initially assembled; rather, new purported facts were introduced whenever it seemed useful to clarify a point, counter a point of the other person, to judge what would happen in a role exchange, etc. This diverse and somewhat unpredictable use of facts made it difficult to be systematic about reducing differences in the most important purported facts. Further, attempts to focus on the purported facts that had been assembled prior to the discussion typically were diverted to other matters which at the moment seemed more important, such as the assessment of the purported fact or some criterion related to it.

We would suggest, then, that in the performance of this task, the moderator follow some systematic procedure for focusing on the most important differences in purported facts assembled. For example, see Steps 2, 3, and 4 of the Procedure for Resolving Value Conflicts described in the next section.

Figure 1. Purported Facts Assembled by Keith and Terry

Keith: Schwartz Plan

Concern R	Negative	Positive	Concern R
PI 1	Some people will quit jobs if they can get almost as much from Schwartz Plan.	34.1 million people below standard would be brought to standard ($3,100/year urban, $1,500 farm).	1 M
E 2	Many people who are in high income public assistance states will get less money.	Does away with other forms of assistance, i.e., public assistance, unemployment. Thus, saving money.	2 PE
P 3	Will probably have more opposition than other plans, i.e., Friedman, Lampman.	If given opportunity to earn salaries more than guarantee, will take it. (Based on Maslow.)	3 PI
E 4	Does not have provision for free medical and dental services.		
P 5	No provision for direct distribution for goods, clothes, etc.		
E 6	Does not take into account locale.		
Ev 7	No historical precedent or research to judge plan by.		
E 8	No tax reforms attached.		

Terry: GMYI Programs

Concern R	Negative	Positive	Concern R
E 1	Implementing HR16311 would cost from 4-7 billion dollars the first year.	Would allow a better standard of living for an estimated 20 million people.	1 E
E 2	Would contribute to inflation and also add another burden to the middle income taxpayers.	HR16311 would establish federal standards of welfare dispensation.	2 E,M
E 3	Would add an estimated 16 million people to tax-supported program rolls.		
P 4	Work incentive programs in New Jersey and Texas (same kind of program to be used in GMYI) have failed.		
E 5	Just another program to add duplicate benefits to existing programs.		
M 6	Accompanying work disincentive would lead to moral decay of society.		

Key: E — Economic   M — Moral   P — Practical   PI — Personal Initiative   Ev — Evidence

3. Reducing Differences in the Assessed Truth of Purported Facts. We devoted little attention to this task for three reasons. One was that we felt there would be little new or clarifying material that would be helpful to the reader. Second, we felt that the limited time would be best devoted to more detailed discussion of the problems with which the reader would be likely to have more difficulty, especially reducing differences in the relevance of facts and in the testing of value principles. Third, both Keith's and Terry's background includes much work in methodology, so that both were aware of standards that have to be met for a purported fact to be assessed as true. Thus, they deleted many items of questionable truth value, and kept for use in the discussion only those purported facts which combined truth value and usefulness.

4. Reducing Differences in the Relevance of Facts. This task involves examining important facts in order to reduce differences in their relevance. We had several examples of reducing differences in relevance, each in a somewhat different way.

The first fact examined was that more people would receive public assistance under the plan. Keith's criterion was "Any plan in which more people receive public assistance under the plan is desirable." Terry's criterion was "Any GMYI plan in which more people receive public assistance is burdensome to the taxpayer." These criteria clearly show that the fact initially had positive valence for Keith and negative valence for Terry. However, after some discussion of the two criteria, it turned out that Keith's criterion did not have much weight since it really doesn't say much, e.g., about how much public assistance the additional people are getting under the plan. Terry pointed out after examining his criterion that it didn't make explicit that there may be more people but they could each be getting less money. Both agreed, then, that their criteria did not take enough circumstances into account. Thus, with essentially the same fact, Keith and Terry had conflicting criteria, but reduced this difference by agreeing that the criteria were not specific enough and so the fact had little relevance for them.

Next, we examined the relevance of Terry's most important fact at this point, that a GMYI plan would cost more, with the criterion "Any plan which costs more than the total of present plans is burdensome." For Keith this criterion was relevant insofar as inflation would eliminate benefits to the poor, but that without being specific about such implications the criterion was not very powerful for him. Thus, some disagreement remained about the relevance of this fact.

We next examined the relevance of Keith's most important positive fact, that the Schwartz plan would bring 34 million people up to a nonpoverty standard, with the criterion "Any program which would raise 34 million people to nonpoverty levels as set forth by the Council of Economic Advisors is desirable." During the discussion of this criterion, Terry inadvertently introduced another fact which touched on his basic economic concern. The moderator's comments illustrate how this might be handled:

K: Anytime all of a formerly poor people can be brought to a nonpoverty level by a program, the program is desirable.

M: OK, so that makes that relevant, very relevant. For you (Terry), that's not relevant.

T: Well, I know what that does. That causes inflation.

M: Wait a minute. Let's look at the criterion, not the result. In the first step you just look at the criterion, and not the result of instituting the plan. Because that's a different fact. What you're doing is bringing in another fact, that the Schwartz plan would result in inflation. That's a separate fact.

T: OK, the way that's set up there is . . . it's significant for me.

Thus, Terry, after seeing that this was a separate fact about a program and that this criterion was to be judged by itself, agreed with the criterion since it expressed his moral concern about the poor. Thus, the initial disagreement about the criterion was reduced by eliminating an oversight, namely bringing in another fact which touched on the economic concern.

The examination of Keith's criterion, described in the previous paragraph, revealed the complexity of the concerns and how the overall decision involved balancing the concerns:

M: A person could hold strictly to the economic picture and say, "Well, I'm sorry, that's not desirable." It's just irrelevant for him, because it doesn't talk about economics. But, this is relevant for you.

T: In the whole decision-making process, it most certainly is.

M: But see, that would make a difference in where you take it from here.

T: It would be easier if it weren't.

M: Well, it's a matter of balancing concerns, rather than just looking at one concern.

T: Yeah.

M: So if you could find a program which would achieve both this kind of thing, raising the standard and satisfying your economic concern, you would look at that. Whereas, and you might give way a little bit on the economic picture because you are concerned with this. But a person who is just concerned with economic would not give way. He would continue to look only at the economic.

Finally, the moderator pointed out that the testing of criteria shows the differences in concerns:

M: This writing of criteria is a good way to test the differences in concern between the two persons. Because when you start asking why do you have the difference in the relevance, the reason is your different concerns. It starts coming out pretty clearly.

5. Reducing Differences in Tentative Value Judgments. A variety of efforts were made to reduce the initial difference in value judgments. However, these were devoted mostly to changing the value object in some way.[8]

The most important was the readjustment of emphasis on the different concerns, especially moral and economic, thus resulting in somewhat different subsidiary value judgments. However, these changes involved changing the value object rather than just the value terms, so we did not follow up on these because of lack of time.

6. Reducing Differences in the Acceptability of Value Principles. To reduce differences in acceptability of value principles, Keith and Terry first stated their value principles. These were written on the board to focus discussion better:

K: Any GMYI which brings 34.1 million people to non-poverty status without nullifying the gain is desirable even though it may result in work disincentive and a rise in prices for nonpoverty levels of income, and even though it probably will have much opposition in Congress.

T: Any GMYI that increases the federal budget from four to seven billion dollars over present proposed budget and adds more people to tax-supported programs and duplicates benefits is undesirable even though it sets national standards for welfare payments and brings a significant number of lower-level income families to nonpoverty level.

The next point that became important was just what we were trying to do in this task. The comments of the moderator helped clarify this point:

M: Well, the idea is to reduce differences. That is, under each kind of test, new cases, role exchange, and so forth. You will each make a set of tests and the idea here would be to, if you can have conflict resolution, to conduct this discussion in such a way that you reduce differences in the way the principle will change. It's just you're looking at it from both points of view, and thinking well, for instance, he may come up with cases that you don't and vice versa. He may come up with — and this will be hard to blame someone, for when you come up with new cases, you're likely to come up with ones positive to the principle. Whereas your opponent more likely would come up with cases against it. So that you're more likely to get a more representative set of cases, by trying to achieve a resolution, say in the role exchange. He may think that the most adverse case is such and such, and you may point out that that's not true at all. Really, the most adverse case is, and so forth. And, then you'd say, "By golly, you're right, I'll test my principle that way." It gets a more common set of experiences to judge your principles by.

M: It's a principle on which you act in a certain class of situations. And that's what you have to figure out here: Am I willing to accept that principle as a guide to my actions in all situations that are covered by the principle?

Since reduction in differences of the acceptability of the principle depends on reducing differences in the ways principles are tested, we turn now to a discussion of the tests for value principles. Since we had no previous experience in conflict resolution, we decided to try the easier tests first. The Role Exchange Test and Universal Consequences Test were done first.

a. *Role Exchange Test.* After recording the two value principles on the board, Keith tested his principle as follows:

The new person would be a person, who say, like in New Jersey, who might get less money with this plan. They've been given a minimum of $3,000, but with this plan they might get cut out of other public assistance and therefore bring the level down . . .

Keith's reaction to being in the role of this kind of person was as follows:

K: My immediate feeling was one of outrage, and as I began to visualize more completely a paradigm of the affected person, other feelings followed in short order. I felt hostility towards the government and then frustration as I realized I couldn't "fight city hall." Finally, this frustration turned to depression as I contemplated the advantages I would lose under the new plan and how this would affect my family's life.

Keith also noted that this was the first thing that occurred to him. He had listed this as one of his negative facts, i.e., that some people now getting public assistance would be dropped if the Schwartz plan were instituted, but did not have this fact represented in the "even though" part of his value principle, the part that has the negative aspects. Although this role exchange was somewhat disturbing, it was not clear how to reformulate the value principle to take care of the difficulty.

Terry's first role exchange was with people in the middle-income level:

> T: Let's talk about the people who are in the middle incomes because there are more of those and the more of those are adversely affected.

Terry's reaction to being in the role of this kind of person was as follows:

> T: I actually identified with the person under role exchange since, in real life, that is my role. This was when the most adversely affected person was the one in the middle income bracket who would foot the bill. My feelings were of righteous indignation and reluctance to spend the money.

After some discussion of who was most adversely affected and what the basis of adversity is, Keith noted that the person most adversely affected is the person who *would have received* benefits if some GMYI were passed. This is because in Terry's principle the GMYI is undesirable, and so would *not* be instituted. Thus those people who would receive benefits under a GMYI would *not* receive benefits under his principle, and so are the most adversely affected under his principle. Terry's reaction to being in the role of this person was as follows:

> T: When the role exchange was with the person who would have received benefits had the plan been instituted, I didn't change my value principle but did empathize with those people. The realization that I might not have enough money to sustain me heightened my moral concern and played down the economic concern. My feelings that prompted this change in concerns included: de-

spair, hostility toward everybody that have more, and anxiety about family well-being.

The impact of this role exchange on Terry's principle illustrates the kind of conflict resolution that can go on without being reflected explicitly in the value judgment or value principle:

M: Well, how do you feel about your principle?

T: I feel like it still stands, pretty much the way it is. However, the more I talk about it, the more the moral concern has than the economic because it'll come out every time we talk about the economy because Keith will bring it up. There's going to be a push-pull type of thing to get funds from somewhere else. I don't really believe that, but there is a possibility. And as long as that possibility exists, then the probability of inflation going down a little bit exists, and also the probability of getting all the money from the "almost poor" group is lessened.

K: So now your concern has come closer and now my statement is something to the effect that even if it did add inflation to the certain upper levels, I would still accept it.

The teacher may want to point out that concern is an important factor in judging who will be most adversely affected. The following comments by the moderator illustrate how this can be done:

M: What's the judgment about adversely affected? Since one of your strong concerns is economics, then you are going to use this concern in saying who is most adversely affected. So, if the plan didn't include all the poor people, certain people would be left out, they wouldn't get any guaranteed income? They would be adversely affected in the sense that now they don't have money to pay their bills, and so forth. Would those most be adversely affected for you, or is it still a case that for you the most adversely affected person is the one above the guaranteed income who is paying the bill? Who is the most adversely affected . . . what's the basis for adverse here?

b. *Universal Consequences Test.* After discussion of the work we had already done, and of a number of characteristics and the appropriate scope of application of the Universal Consequences Test, we decided that it would not be of much help in testing the two value principles.

c. *New Cases Test.* In the New Cases Test we tested Keith's principle by considering a GMYI plan with all the characteristics in his value principle but in addition it would result in some kind of economic disaster. Since he considered this so unlikely, even giving reasons for it being unlikely, he did not modify his value principle as a result of the test. However, it would be easy to modify the principle by adding the phrase ". . . even though there is a small possibility of some kind of economic disaster occurring."[9]

d. *Subsumption Test.* We had no time to use this test. However, if we had had the time, we would have considered some more general principles such as "Government programs which are inflationary are harmful to the country" and its corresponding fact, "GMYI programs would duplicate benefits and produce inflation" and the general principle "Attempts to reduce poverty are morally right" and its corresponding fact, "GMYI programs dispense billions of dollars to poverty-stricken people in an attempt to reduce poverty." Each person would identify a sufficient number of these more general principles and their corresponding facts to enable him to deduce from all this the value principle being tested. A comparison of the general principles of Keith and Terry might have revealed considerable similarity in their principles, and suggested facts that could be used to connect these general principles to the value principles being tested or suggested ways to modify these value principles so as to make them more similar.

Principles for Resolving Value Conflict

In the preceding sections of this chapter we have discussed a variety of techniques and strategies a teacher could employ to help students resolve value conflicts. The same kinds of decisions were left open to the teacher in this chapter as in Chapter 2, e.g., the amount and kind of effort on each task, the order in which the teacher wants the students to pursue the tasks, and the extent and kind of his own participation in the conflict resolution. In Chapter 3 we were able to present some specific step-by-step procedures which specify teacher activity for some of these decisions, procedures which we had tried in the classroom with considerable success. However, we do not have a comparable amount of experience with resolving value conflict. Thus, since our experience with strategies and procedures for resolving value conflicts is very limited, we are proposing a number of general principles that we have already used or that seem reasonable. We have divided these principles into logical, procedural, and psychological principles. The teacher may select and combine these principles in a variety of ways to formulate his own strategies and procedures.

I. LOGICAL PRINCIPLES

Four principles seem important.

1. *Analyze value conflict into its logical components.* Logical components could be identified in terms of the five sources of conflict discussed in Chapter 1, the six tasks discussed in Chapter 2, or the Extended Model discussed in Chapter 3. We discuss both the second and third approaches in this chapter.

2. *Differentiate logical components of the value analysis to reduce differences.* Once the logical components have been identified, they may be further differentiated to reduce conflict. For example, comparison classes in criteria may be differentiated by narrowing them to reduce differences, or general value terms may be differentiated into more specific value terms to reduce differences. Specific examples are given in the discussion below of the task "Arriving at a Tentative Value Decision."

3. *Reinterpret value objects, criteria, principles, and situations to reduce differences.* Reinterpreting a value object may

help reduce conflict by associating the object with another class of things that has a different value. For example, if fluoridation is the value object or issue, with one person interpreting or classifying it as compulsory medication and the other person interpreting or classifying it as a public health measure, it would reduce differences if both persons interpreted fluoridation as a chemical added to the public water supply.

4. *Appeal to epistemic rules wherever relevant.* The appeal to epistemic rules involves an appeal to the rules of evidence and scientific method, definitional rules, rules of deductive argument, rules of testimony, and the like. Such an appeal should help reduce differences by helping both persons be more accurate and sound in their value analysis.

II. PROCEDURAL PRINCIPLES

These procedural principles are simple extensions of some of the suggestions for handling complexity in Chapter 2 and the procedures used in the Rudimentary Procedure and the Extended Procedure described in Chapter 3.

1. *Identify the sources of conflict.* Each person may work by himself in identifying the sources, or the two persons can work together. The sources of the conflict can be identified in logical terms, psychological terms, in historical terms, etc.

2. *Rank the sources of conflict with respect to their importance.* The sources of conflict identified can be ranked by each person separately, and can also be ranked jointly by the two persons. The joint ranking is more likely to clarify which sources of conflict would most fruitfully be resolved first.

3. *Organize the sources of conflict using the Fact-Assembly Chart and Evidence Cards described in Chapter 2.* In addition to listing and ranking sources of conflict, it should help the two persons resolve their conflict if they can see the relations among the sources and what part they play in the overall value judgments.

III. PSYCHOLOGICAL PRINCIPLES

A variety of psychological principles for resolving conflict can be found in the literature. However, since there is inadequate research to support most of them, especially as they might be extended to resolving value conflict, we shall propose only four principles, all of which seem relatively reasonable for use in resolving value conflict. The principles are intended to help the person achieve some "progress" in a conflict resolution. This progress should increase satisfaction with efforts at resolving value conflict and encourage future attempts at resolving value conflict.

1. *Resolve easy conflicts before hard conflicts.* One conflict may be easier to resolve than another conflict because of any of a number of factors. One factor is the size of the conflict; another is the importance of the conflict. Thus the next two principles may be regarded as special cases of this first principle.

2. *Break larger conflicts into smaller conflicts, resolving the smaller conflicts first.* Smaller conflicts are typically easier to resolve than larger ones (Deutsch, 1969). For example, it should be easier to resolve a conflict between two individuals of different races than a general racial conflict; and it should be easier to resolve a conflict over being treated fairly on a particular occasion than a conflict over being treated fairly in general.

3. *Resolve conflicts involving "shell" values before conflicts involving "core" values.* It will typically be much more difficult to resolve conflicts involving "core" values — those values most important to the person — than conflicts involving "shell" values — those values least important to the person.[10] For example, as Deutsch (1969) suggests, conflicts which involve self-esteem, changes in power or status, or religious values are likely to be of central importance to the person. If some progress can be made on the conflicts involving "shell" values, this may encourage the two persons to resolve the conflicts involving the "core" values. Also it may turn out that "core" values are relatively unimportant for the particular value conflict at hand.

4. *Maintain good will and intention to resolve the value conflict in order to increase the probability of achieving a rational resolution of the value conflict.* The importance of this principle is to remind the persons attempting to resolve a value conflict to maintain conditions which allow them to maintain good will. Deutsch (1969) indicates a variety of factors which influence these conditions, both positively and negatively. Examples of these factors are cooperative processes, prior relationships, illegitimate threats, availability of diverse ideas, and the use of excessive influence.

A Procedure for Resolving Value Conflicts

The procedure for resolving value conflicts described here incorporates a number of the principles discussed above. The most important of these principles are: Logical Principles 1 and 4; Procedural Principles 1, 2, and 3; and Psychological Principles 2 and 4.

Although this procedure has not been tested to the same extent as the Extended Procedure described in Chapter 3, there are a number of similarities — e.g., the use of the Procedural Principles — that would seem to increase the likelihood of the procedure here being successful.

The use of this procedure assumes that the two persons have gone through the Extended Procedure described in Chapter 3, or at least steps 1, 2, 4, and 5, if just conflict in the value judgments on the initial *topic* is to be resolved. If value judgments on *solutions* are to be resolved, then the entire Extended Procedure will be needed, or at least steps 10, 11, and 14 (the solution phase). In addition to the steps in the Extended Procedure, each of the two persons will also need to formulate his value principle. We also recommend highly the use of a blackboard.

We present here selected parts of an actual conflict resolution on one proposed solution to the population problem, liberalization of abortion. Conditions were similar to the GMYI example: Keith and Janet, two graduate students in educational psychology, were the participants, the discussion was moderated by the author, and was taped, transcribed, and edited for the purposes of clarity and coherence. Each person had read on the issue and followed most of the steps in the Extended Procedure, and had formulated a value principle. We also used the blackboard.

STEP 1. *Record Initial Value Judgments.* The two persons first record their value judgments, as in Figure 2. This step may include simple clarifying comments.

STEP 2. *Comparing and Modifying Positive and Negative Statements.* The two persons compare their lists of ranked positive and negative statements that they have already prepared in order to reduce any differences that may have occurred through oversight, not reading the same sources, and the like. This step should provide the two persons an opportunity to start off with as common a set of statements as possible. This step will probably take 5 to 10 minutes.

Figure 2 contains the positive and negative statements of Keith and Janet. The initial statements are not underlined, whereas the statements added as a result of the comparison are underlined. (Rather than underlining, different colored pencils could be used.) Although Figure 2 contains material from both persons for purposes of comparison, in actual practice the two persons keep their material separate.

STEP 3. *Ranking the Modified Positive and Negative Statements.* As a result of the first step, the two persons will very likely have a modified set of positive and negative statements. In this third step, each person ranks his own new set of statements. Figure 2 includes both the initial rankings (R_1) and the reranking (R_2) after the underlined statements were added.

STEP 4. *Identifying Important Sources of Conflict.* Perhaps the most important source of conflict in the purported facts would be a purported fact which has positive valence for one person and negative valence for the other person, and which has a high ranking for each person. Such a purported fact can be identified by examining the lists of positive and negative statements, and identifying each high-ranking statement that is positive for one person and negative for the other person.

A second important source of conflict in the purported facts

Figure 2. Initial and Modified Positive and Negative Statements and Rankings

KEITH

Initial VJ: Liberalization of abortion is highly desirable.

R₂	R₁	NEGATIVE	POSITIVE	R₁	R₂
1	1	Religious objections due to controversy over when we begin to call something a human being.	Would reduce births beyond former numbers what would otherwise be expected.	1	1
2	2	Cultural objections for other reasons than statement 1.	Abortion, properly performed, is not as dangerous as a normal childbirth.	2	2
3	3	Cost of a comprehensive plan, especially in underdeveloped countries.	Abortion per se causes no psychological damage.	3	3
			Would reduce proportion of children raised by resentful mothers.	4	5
			No discrimination against poor because of illegal abortions.		5

JANET

Initial VJ: Liberalization of abortion is undesirable.

R₂	R₁	NEGATIVE	POSITIVE	R₁	R₂
1	1	We do not know when what society has called ~~life~~ a human being begins.	Abortion is the only post-conception control acceptable to large numbers of people.	1	1
2	2	Abortion is morally unacceptable to many people.	Abortion is becoming an increasingly uncomplicated and safe operation.	2	2
3	3	The problem of control is more motivational than technological.	Abortion would reduce the proportion of children being raised by resentful mothers.		3
4	3	Abortion is culturally and traditionally objectionable to some people.	Abortion per se causes no psychological damage.		4

Key: Underlining— statements or phrases added in Step 2.
Word crossed out indicates deletion during Step 2.
R₁ — Initial ranking before discussion.
R₂ — Reranking in Step 3.

would be a purported fact which has positive valence for one person and no valence for the other person, or a purported fact which has negative valence for one person and no valence for the other person. Since there are likely to be quite a few of these, it will save time to identify for each person only the top-ranked statements that do not appear on the other person's list of statements at all. Thus, the first person finds his highest-ranked positive statement that does not appear on the second person's list of statements at all, then finds his highest-ranked negative statement that does not appear on the second person's list of statements at all. Then the second person finds his highest-ranked positive statement that does not appear on the first person's list of statements at all, then finds the highest-ranked negative statement that does not appear on the first person's list of statements at all.[11]

All the statements identified so far are recorded on the blackboard or on paper to provide a focus for future steps. The statements of Keith and Janet identified in this step are contained in Figure 3.

Figure 3. **Identification of Statements Most Likely to Produce Conflict**

Keith	Janet	Initial Statement (at start of Step 4)	Modified Statement (at end of Step 4)
+	−	None	Would reduce expected birth rate significantly beyond what it would have been
−	+	None	None
+	O	Liberalized abortion would reduce births beyond former number	Deleted
O	+	Abortion is the only post-conception control acceptable to large numbers of people	Abortion is the only post-conception control acceptable to large numbers of people
−	O	Religious objections due to controversy over when we begin to call something a human being	Liberalized abortion involves destroying life which is in the range about which there is controversy about the meaning of the term "human being"
O	−	We do not know when what society has called a human being begins	

Key: +: Top ranked positive statement
    −: Top ranked negative statement
    O: Statement is not included in this person's list

In the process of identifying the statements, reformulations may occur. For example, in locating statements which were positive for Keith and negative for Janet, both of them noted that Keith's top ranked positive statement — "Would reduce births beyond . . ." — was in conflict with an *implication* of Janet's third-ranked negative statement — "The problem of control is more motivational than technological . . ." — i.e., that birth rate would not be reduced significantly by liberalized abortion. After some discussion, this statement was reformulated to read "Would reduce expected birth rate significantly beyond what it would have been." This modified statement is recorded in Figure 3. (Further, discussion indicated that for Janet this statement is negative in the sense that she contends that liberalized abortion would not reduce birth rate significantly beyond what it would have been.) This modification then resulted in the deletion of the statement "Liberalized abortion would reduce births beyond former number" that was positive for Keith and not on Janet's list, since it is the same as the reformulated statement. The second modification occurred when both Keith and Janet noted that the bottom two statements in Figure 3 involved essentially the same thing about the controversy over the meaning of the term "human being," and that this was therefore not a source of conflict. Thus both the statements were deleted from the modified list.

STEP 5. *Comparing and Modifying Evidence Cards for Most Important Sources of Conflict.* A complete treatment of the purported facts to assess their truth and to clarify their relevance would involve writing an Evidence Card — or its equivalent — for each of the statements identified in the previous step. This should help reduce differences by deleting statements which have little or no evidence and by clarifying the concerns reflected in the selection and ranking of the purported facts. Discussion of the criteria may result in a variety of modifications that could reduce conflict.

Figure 4 contains the facts identified in the previous step, initial criteria written for these facts identified in the previous step, and the criteria as they were modified after discussion.[12] One change was in Keith's comparison class and value term —

Person	Fact Identified in Step 4	Initial Criterion (at start of Step 5)	Modified Criterion (at end of Step 5)
Keith	Liberalized abortion reduces birth rate beyond what it would be	Any birth control procedure which is voluntary, ethical and rational, and effective is desirable	Any birth control procedure that reduces birth rate is effective
Janet	Liberalized abortion is acceptable to large numbers of people	Any post-conception control acceptable to large numbers of people is feasible	Same
Keith and Janet	Liberalized abortion has religious and cultural objections	Any birth control procedure which has religious and cultural objections is less feasible	Same
Janet	Liberalized abortion has religious and cultural objections	Any birth control procedure which has religious and cultural objections is unethical	Same
Janet	Liberalized abortion does not take into account the fact that we don't know when human life begins	Any birth control procedure which does not take into account the fact that we don't know when human life begins is unethical	Any birth control procedure which destroys life in the range about which there is controversy about the meaning of "human being" is unethical

Figure 4. **Facts, Initial Criteria, and Modified Criteria for Statements Most Likely to Produce Conflict**

rather than try to include all the characteristics of a birth control procedure which would make it desirable, he focused only on that feature which would make it effective, i.e., reducing the birth rate. Second, Keith and Janet came closer together on the criterion "Any birth control procedure which has religious and cultural objections is less feasible." However, Keith clearly disagreed with Janet on the criterion "Any birth control procedure which destroys life in the range about which there is controversy about the meaning of 'human being' is unethical."

STEP 6. *Ranking Modified List of Positive and Negative Statements.* After the previous step the two persons may wish to rerank their positive and negative statements. This will help them in deciding whether to modify their value principles.

STEP 7. *Comparing and Modifying Value Principles.* Considerable discussion in the procedure up to this point will have been relevant to modifying each person's value principle. Although some explicit modification may have occurred — as was the case with Keith and Janet — this step provides an opportunity to integrate the various points that have been made up to this point, and to bring up more by focusing explicitly on the value principle. Figure 5 contains for both Keith and Janet the initial value principle brought to the conflict resolution and the modified value principle resulting from this step.

STEP 8. *Comparing Tests for Modified Value Principles.* The two persons now test their modified value principles, using whatever tests for their value principles have been brought to the conflict resolution, and new tests which result from working together on the modified value principles. The two persons help each other in their tests in much the same way as was discussed under Task 6 in the previous section, e.g., in finding the most adverse cases in the role exchange for the other person's principle.

In the Role Exchange Test, it was decided that the most adversely affected person under Keith's value principle would be either a staunch Catholic woman or a woman in an underdeveloped country such as India where such a program might

Person	Initial Value Principle (Before Discussion)	Modified Value Principle (from Step 7)	Final Value Principle (from Step 9)
Keith	Any birth control program which has no Hitler-type connotations, is voluntary, would reduce births beyond what they otherwise would be, is safer than normal childbirth, and would cause no psychological damage is highly desirable even though there are religious and cultural objections due to controversy over when to begin calling something a human being and even though it may be very costly especially in under-developed countries.	No change.	Any birth control program which has no Hitler-type connotation, is voluntary, would reduce births beyond what they would otherwise be, is safer than normal childbirth, and might prevent other more drastic, involuntary measures from being taken later, is highly desirable even though there are religious and cultural objections over when to begin to call something a human being, it may be very costly, but not to the extent of depriving the family of other necessities, and it may cause some psychological damage.
Janet	Any birth control procedure that is unethical and has not been shown to be significantly more effective for population control than educational programs alone is undesirable even though it is technologically feasible and may be acceptable to large numbers of people.	Any birth control procedure that involves the HB controversy, and has not been shown to be significantly more effective for population control than educational programs is undesirable even though it is technologically feasible and may be acceptable to large numbers of people.	Any birth control procedure that involves disobeying L.D.S. descriptions of law, and has not been shown to be significantly more effective for population control than educational programs is extremely undesirable even though it is technologically feasible and may be acceptable to large numbers of people.

Figure 5. Comparing Initial and Modified Value Principles of Keith and Janet

cost a prohibitive amount. It was decided that the most adversely affected person under Janet's value principle would be a pregnant woman with no particular religion and no feelings about the controversy about the meaning of "human being" and who might commit suicide with another child added to an already large family.

The results of the other three kinds of tests may be stated briefly. The Universal Consequences Test did not seem particularly helpful. We could not seem to think of any new cases for the New Cases Test — we had already discussed the issue from so many angles we could not think of anything new. We did not have time to do the Subsumption Test explicitly, although there were times during the discussion where higher level (more general) principles were invoked, such as the descriptions of Mormon law.

STEP 9. *Revising Value Principles.* This step provides a last opportunity, after testing the modified value principles, for each person to revise his value principle. The final principles for Keith and Janet are contained in Figure 5.

STEP 10. *Comparing Final Value Judgments.* This last step is just a final check on the extent to which there has been any conflict resolved in the value judgments themselves; in other words, whether there has been any change in the value judgments as a result of the previous comparisons and modifications of facts, criteria, and principles. In our conflict resolution, there was actually an increase in the value conflict — with Janet going from an initial value judgment of "Liberalization of abortion is undesirable" to a final value judgment of "Liberalization of abortion is extremely undesirable." Keith's value judgment stayed the same: "Liberalization of abortion is highly desirable."

Comments on Objectives and Outcomes in Resolving Value Conflicts

There is a serious question as to what the criteria are for a successful resolution of a value conflict, a question which is somewhat more difficult than might first appear. This matter was discussed briefly in Chapter 1. It is true that if the persons agree on the same value judgment that this would seem to be a successful resolution. However, if the same value judgment is not agreed upon, is this automatically to be judged a failure? Perhaps not, as the following considerations indicate.

There may be a fundamental conflict between being rational and achieving a complete resolution of a value conflict (i.e., both persons agreeing on the same value judgment). Suppose that both persons have carried out the six tasks described in Chapter 2 (or used the Extended Procedure described in Chapter 3) so as to meet the standards for a rational value judgment in Chapter 1, and have decided on value judgments which conflict. It may be that the factors in the value situation that resulted in the conflicting value judgments in the first place would still operate so as to prevent a complete resolution of the value conflict. It seems unlikely that the two persons — or even objective observers — would be able to predict in detail what the factors would be that would prevent a complete resolution, and just how much and what kind of resolution might take place. Because of these considerations the two persons attempting to resolve their value conflict should not judge their efforts to be a failure if a complete resolution is not achieved. Although we are not prepared to offer a justifiable set of criteria for successful value conflict resolutions, we propose the following kinds of outcomes be considered as partial yet important resolutions.

The lack of a resolution in value conflict may be only or mostly on the initial value object so that the resolution appears more clearly on closely related objects. (1) The reduction of differences in value principles might result in reduction of differences in evaluation of a variety of other value objects that come under the new value principles. (2) The initial value object may represent an attempt at a solution of some problem, and what is needed is a better solution. The initial value conflict may be retained but the persons may find new value objects which do not elicit as strong a conflict. We found repeated attempts to find better solutions or at least agree on the criteria for better solutions, as indicated in the following comments.

M : Yes, but suppose it takes people off tax-supported programs. You could start changing things in there that wouldn't be covered by your principle.

T : You know, that's very good because let's say, now I'm going to get a big fight between economics here and morals. So I'll say that my GMYI that increases the federal budget from two billion dollars over the present proposed budget and doesn't add more people's tax-supported incomes. Let's just say it doesn't add. Now, I might say that's desirable. . . .

M : Ok, now, are those two conditions that Keith put forth — would you consider those, if those were met would the plan be acceptable?

T : Specify the conditions.

K : The conditions are (1) that it will raise, solve the problem of raising of urban families of $3130 a year and farm families of $2190 a year, and (2) is that it won't bring about more than a 5 percent rise in cost of living attributable to the plan. So we won't get inflation out of it so their money will be useless.

The two persons may find that their final value judgments are closer or more similar than the initial value judgments even though complete agreement cannot be achieved at present.

The two persons may find that some but not all of the sources of the conflict can be resolved, even though the overall conflict in the initial value judgments has not changed.

The persons may reduce their differences in a variety of ways, such as finding more facts in common as a basis for their value judgments, finding that they are closer than they thought on their basic concerns, finding more criteria of relevance to both persons, and more similar value principles. Of course, there may also be an increase in differences as we experienced with Keith and Janet. This feeling of almost simultaneous decrease and increase in a variety of differences was well expressed by Terry:

> T: I would like to say that at different points in this procedure we're closer together than we are at other points, and it doesn't necessarily mean we are funneling — maybe a scalloping effect . . . then something new comes up and that takes us further apart again.

The two persons may agree that both initial value judgments were unsound or inadequate, and that more research, information, or experience is needed before a sound value judgment can be formulated.

Each person may believe that his final value judgment is sounder and more rational than his initial value judgment. Thus, there might be some reduction in the value conflict, and it may be the maximum possible reduction while still retaining *rational* value judgments. Further reduction or resolution of the value conflict would require one or both persons to depart from the standards of rationality.[13]

Even though there may not be much explicit reduction in conflict between the two persons, there may be considerable reduction in conflict *within* each person. Any controversial issue that is important to a person will engage two or more of his basic concerns that conflict. For Terry in the GMYI issue it was the conflict between his economic concern and his moral concern. The formulation of criteria and the testing of his value principle helped clarify the relative importance of these two concerns for him. This point may be stated in terms of interperson and intraperson conflict: although the objective of the conflict resolution is resolution of interperson conflict, there may be more resolution of *intra*person conflict than *inter*person conflict.

It is important to realize that in real life situations, the reduction of value conflict is only one aspect of a total effort to resolve conflict. Compromise, bargaining, and negotiation on *specific* courses of action, policies, etc., are involved. Thus, even if there may be little reduction in value conflict in the initial value judgments, what reduction of difference that does occur may be reflected in greater ease of achieving a compromise that will reflect and strengthen the points of agreement now made explicit and minimize the points of disagreement that still remain. This point, of course, is closely related to the third point, since the urge to achieve better solutions is common to both.

Finally, the attempt at conflict resolution may result in an increased understanding of and respect for the other person, a kind of "getting below the surface." The following comment expresses this:

> T: Do you know what I think this conflict resolution comes from? You take a main issue (it's pretty hard to resolve a main issue), but you get down into the smaller things and you start agreeing about those, and you build a little rapport there — getting to know how the other person feels. . . . And that's a whole lot of it.

A closely related point is that efforts to resolve value conflict help achieve a deeper realization that we all have deep commitments that deserve consideration and respect, and that to ignore this phenomenon can have ominous and sinister implications for our society.

NOTES

[1] Although the relations between the various kinds of conflict, including value conflict, are complex, two points are interesting. (1) The concept of value conflict as we use it here is related to a historically important concept of conflict due to Lewin (1931, 1935). It is an important feature of conflict that two or more courses of action are involved, and the person can take only one course of action. Thus there is a directional sense to conflict — one approaches or avoids an object or course of action, so that when one is in conflict he is faced with a choice as to what is most desirable. This directional aspect is also present in values, for one of the most important features of values is that they are directional. If we value something positively, we will act so as to move toward it, maintain it, bring it into existence, etc. If we disvalue something, we will act so as to move away from it, reduce it, destroy it, etc. Although value conflict may get complicated, we can at least say about it that typically something is being evaluated both positively in some way and negatively in some way. (2) The connection between conflict in general and value conflict in particular is also brought out in Sisson and Ackoff's conception of conflict: "One party, A, is in *conflict* with

another, B, if A affects the outcome of B's behavior and the value of this outcome to B is less than that of the outcome that would have occurred if B [sic] had not affected it." (1966, p. 126). (They clearly mean A, not B.)

[2] Of course, to the extent to which there is inadequate evidence to assess the truth of a purported fact, each person's opinion about the truth will tend to prevail.

[3] The latter is often the case in trying to decide on which solution or course of action to select, and the most relevant facts would involve what happens when the solution is adopted; but there is often little direct evidence to support such purported factual assertions.

[4] We assume here, as in Chapter 2, that each person does understand that value judgments do rest on principles, that principles can be tested for their soundness, and changed accordingly.

[5] This general answer would need some amplification for differences between the four kinds of tests for principles in general on any topic or issue or differences between the two persons as to which of the tests is most appropriate in a particular value conflict. However, attempts to reduce these two kinds of differences should probably be made only after more detailed consideration of how to reduce the differences that arise within each of the four tests.

[6] Thus differences in the value principles, differences in the acceptability of value principles, and differences in the testing of value principles are all essentially the same thing.

[7] A particular plan, a member of the class of GMYI's with such features as a $3,000 maximum subsidy to a family of four and a high rate of tax on any income over the subsidized amount.

[8] See the discussion below in the section on Comments on Objectives and Outcomes in Conflict Resolution.

[9] One interesting point was that in the discussion of this case Keith thought it very unlikely that there could be an extreme consequence of a GMYI plan like the one in his principle; rather, he thought it much more likely that the extreme consequence of not having a GMYI plan could occur, i.e., some kind of moral decay, loss of hope for millions of people, and the like. Terry, on the other hand, thought it very unlikely that there would be an extreme consequence of not having a GMYI plan; rather he thought it much more likely that there could be an extreme consequence of a GMYI plan such as in Keith's principle. These beliefs seemed to be based largely on the strengths of their concerns.

[10] This terminology due to Boulding (1962).

[11] Of course, if there is time, second-ranked statements which do not appear on the other person's list, third-ranked statements, etc., may be taken.

[12] This is essentially the same information as is contained on simple Evidence Cards. It is easier, however, to present here in this form.

[13] Such departures from standards of rationality could mean that the person would be subjected to the use of a variety of techniques such as pressures to conformity, threats, cajolery, subtle persuasion, and direct coercion.

READINGS AND REFERENCES IN CONFLICT RESOLUTION

Boulding, K. E. *Conflict and Defense: A General Theory.* New York: Harper and Row, 1962.

Coser, L. *The Functions of Social Conflict.* New York: The Free Press, 1956.

Deutsch, M. "Conflicts: Productive and Destructive," *Journal of Social Issues,* 1969, *25,* Pp. 7-41.

Kaplan, B., and W. H. Crockett. "Developmental Analysis of Modes of Resolution." In R. P. Abelson, *et. al.* (eds.), *Theories of Cognitive Consistency: A Sourcebook.* Chicago: Rand McNally, 1968. Pp. 661-669.

Kelman, H. C., and R. M. Baron. "Determinants of Modes of Resolving Inconsistency Dilemmas: a Functional Analysis." In R. P. Abelson, *et. al.* (eds.), *Theories of Cognitive Consistency: A Sourcebook.* Chicago: Rand McNally, 1968. Pp. 670-683.

Lewin, K. "Environmental Forces in Child Behavior and Development." In C. Murchison (ed.), *A Handbook of Child Psychology.* Worcester, Mass.: Clark University Press, 1931.

Lewin, K. *A Dynamic Theory of Personality.* New York: McGraw-Hill, 1935.

McNeil, E. G. (ed.), *The Nature of Human Conflict.* Englewood Cliffs, New Jersey: Prentice-Hall, 1965.

Miller, D. R., and G. E. Swanson. *Inner Conflict and Defense.* New York: Schocken Books, 1966.

Mudd, S. (ed.), *Conflict Resolution and World Education.* The Hague: Dr. W. Junk Publishers, 1966.

Oliver, D. W., and J. P. Shaver. *Teaching Public Issues in the High School.* Boston: Houghton-Mifflin, 1966.

Raths, L. E., M. Harmin, and S. B. Simon. *Values and Teaching.* Columbus, Ohio: Charles E. Merrill, 1966.

Raup, B. R., G. E. Axtelle, K. D. Benne, and B. O. Smith. *The Improvement of Practical Intelligence.* New York: Harper and Brothers, 1943.

Sisson, R. L., and R. L. Ackoff. "Toward a Theory of the Dynamics of Conflict." In S. Mudd (ed.), *Conflict Resolution and World Education.* The Hague: Dr. W. Junk Publishers, 1966. Pp. 125-142.

Appendix

Procedure for Personal Interviews

A Value Model: A Programmed Text

Procedure for Personal Interviews

JAMES CHADWICK

NOTE: *This section contains a brief description of the study in which the personal interview was developed, together with a description of the procedure itself.*

Purpose of the Study

The purposes of the study were: (1) to conduct personal interviews between teachers and students and administrators and students, (2) to develop a procedure for personal interviews that would decrease imposition of viewpoints and increase honest reaction.

The personal interview is a potent and indispensable tool, yielding data that no other tool can yield. It is capable of being used with all kinds of respondents in all kinds of situations and is uniquely suited to exploration in depth. Until the two major weaknesses, imposition of interviewer bias and inhibition of honest interviewee reaction, are reduced significantly, the personal interview will continue to be of limited value.

Procedure

The procedure used in this study involved an initial study to develop an interview procedure and a final study to test the procedure. The instruments used were semantic differential, questionnaire, and audio and video tape recordings.

Initial Study

1. The initial group of 30 teachers was divided into two equal groups. The workshop group was trained in an initial interviewing procedure based on outside sources and the workshop's methodology. The nonworkshop group was not trained in any procedure.

2. Ninety public school students were divided into six equal groups and were rotated so that every student was interviewed by a member of each group.

3. Each nonworkshop interviewer (1) took a pre-interview semantic differential, (2) conducted the interview, (3) took a post-interview semantic differential, and (4) responded to a post-interview questionnaire.

4. Based on the data collected from the initial interviews, the personal interviewing procedure was developed.

Final Study

The interviewers in the final study were 25 administrators who were Educational Administration students. They were assigned to three groups randomly. The first two groups contained 10 members each. The trained group was trained in the procedure and the untrained group was not trained in the procedure but allowed to read it. The other five members were assigned to the comparison group, which had no contact with the procedure.

Results

The results of the final study showed that the comparison group interviewees moved toward the interviewers at a 3.2:1 ratio. (A move is defined as a change on the pre-interview to the post-interview semantic differential of at least one scale position on the seven point scale.) In the untrained group, the interviewees moved toward the interviewer at a 0.9:1 ratio, and in the trained group, the interviewees moved toward the interviewer at a 0.3:1 ratio.

In the comparison group, the ratio of minutes of ·interviewer to interviewee talking time was 3.4:1. In the untrained group, the ratio of interviewer to interviewee talking time was 0.9:1. In the trained group, the ratio of interviewer to inter· viewee talking time was 0.2:1.

A review of the video tapes indicated that no more than one interviewing procedural technique, any heading or subheading in the description of the procedure, was used by any of the comparison group interviewers. The untrained group averaged about seventeen interviewing procedural techniques out of a possible twenty-nine.

Conclusions

It was found that there was imposition of viewpoint in the interview. If an interviewer imposed his viewpoint, the interviewee's honest reaction decreased. If an interviewer read the interviewing procedure and incorporated the techniques, he would decrease interviewer imposition of viewpoint and increase interviewee reaction approximately four times more than the interviewer who had had no previous contact with the interviewing procedure. If an interviewer was trained in the interviewing procedure and incorporated its techniques into the interview, he decreased interviewer imposition of viewpoint and increased interviewee reaction approximately eleven times more than the interviewer who had had no previous contact with the interviewing procedure.

The Interview Procedure

A. *Preparation for the Interview*

    1. The interviewer should not only determine but define his purpose for using the interview in obtaining the information required. This should include clarification in thinking and writing as to what actually is to be served by the interview; planning a step-by-step agenda as to what facts must be brought out, what information must be given, what attitudes should be established, and what action is to be taken.

    2. The interviewer should attempt to clarify his preconceived points of view about the topic.

    3. The interviewer should place himself in the interviewee's position and try to imagine what the interviewee would think of the interviewer, the approach, and the purposes of the interview.

B. *The Interview*

    1. The interviewer should set the mood for the interview by explaining that it will be based upon a mutual understanding of its purposes. Thus, the interviewee should see that by his participating in the interview he could help to achieve some goal or bring about some change which he considered desirable.

2. The interview begins when agreement on a purpose has been reached between the interviewer and the interviewee. From this point on, the interviewer must tread a fine line with respect to his responsiveness. It was essential that the interviewer try not to reveal his own attitudes — including not showing shock or disapproval or nodding support. However, the interviewer must not become completely impassive. The interviewer should compromise by adopting a manner of friendly permissiveness. For example, he should laugh at the interviewee's jokes, exclaim when the interviewee says something evidently intended to be astonishing ("Really?"; "You don't say!"), make supportive statements ("I see your point," "That's understandable," "That's very interesting"), and in any other way allow himself the appropriate emotional expression which would be normal for the particular situation. But, the interviewer should avoid the slightest approval or disapproval of the interviewee's positions.

3. The interviewer should be a good listener, which means he should actively participate through concentrated effort to examine and comprehend the true meaning of what the interviewee is trying to communicate.

4. The interviewer should let the interviewee tell his own story. Then after the interviewee has had a chance to give the main story, uninterrupted by questioning, the interviewer should complete the interview by questioning him about any incomplete portion of it.

5. The interviewer should ask only one question at a time, and his wording should be such that the meaning is clear. The following are some suggestions about questioning and wording:

   a. The interviewer should ask only questions that are related to the purposes of the interview.

   b. The interviewer should avoid using leading questions because they suggest answers.

   c. The interviewer should not use questions that are loaded with social desirability. People tend to give responses that are socially desirable, responses that indicate or imply approval of actions or things that are generally considered to be good. For example, the interviewer may ask a person about his feelings toward children. Everybody is supposed to love children. Unless the interviewer is very careful, he will get a stereotyped response about children and love. Also, when the interviewer asks a person if he votes, he must be careful since everyone is supposed to vote. If he asks interviewees their reactions to minority groups, he again runs the risk of getting invalid responses. Most educated people, no matter what their true attitudes, are aware that prejudice is disapproved. A good question, then, is one in which interviewees are not led to express merely socially desirable sentiments. At the same time, one should not question an interviewee so that he is faced with the necessity of giving a socially undesirable response.

d. Make questions short enough so that the interviewee will be able to remember them.

e. Specify, as close as possible, the exact time, place, and context which you desire the interviewee to assume when he answers your questions.

f. Questions should be worded so that a single "Yes" or "No" answer is not possible unless there is no other way.

g. When the interview concerns a subject with which the interviewee may not be very familiar, or one in which he may not have the necessary technical vocabulary, it is sometimes desirable to preface questions with an explanatory paragraph or an illustration which will set the stage for the question the interviewer wants to ask.

h. Ask questions in terms of the interviewee's own immediate (recent) experience, rather than in terms of generalities. For example, the interviewer can ask, "Think back to the last time one of your students came in late. What did you say?", rather than "What do you usually say when a student comes in late?"

i. When the interview deals with sensitive topics, attention must be given to wording questions in such a way as to minimize ego defenses. This can be accomplished by making the interviewee's desired answer seem acceptable. The following are some ways in which this can be accomplished:

(1) If the sensitive area involves the expression of criticism of a person or institution, provide an opportunity for the interviewee to voice praise first, so that he will not feel he is being unfair. For example, "What do you like best about your teacher?", then "What do you like least about your teacher?"

(2) Indicate to the interviewee that other people hold the same opinion even though it's not socially acceptable.

(3) If the interviewer feels it necessary to discuss some undesirable attitude or behavior of the interviewee, he

should place the burden of denial on him. For example, "When did you first sluff school?" instead of "Did you ever sluff school?"

(4) Introduce face-saving phrases and words. For example, "Do you happen to know who the principal of this school is?" instead of "Do you know . . .?"

(5) Too often unintentional criticism is conveyed through mere disappointment over the fact that the interviewee failed to touch upon certain matters which the interviewer felt pertinent to the success of the interview. However expressed, the interviewee sees it as a personal indictment.

(6) In general, it seems preferable to have a further question directed to the affective aspects of what is being said rather than to pounce upon a factually inaccurate statement. Few devices are better calculated to stem the flow of conversation than that of countering an apparent statement of fact, which is actually the expression of a sentiment, with proof that the alleged fact is not true.

6. When continued self-exploration becomes uncomfortable, the interviewer should be aware of the fact that interviewees often attempt to reverse their roles. For example, he may be reluctant to explore his own feelings because they are painful or embarrassing or because they are so diffuse that he cannot easily put them into words. Whatever the reasons, he hopes that the interviewer's answer will provide the "correct" formulation of his own vague feelings. When this situation arises, it is important that the interviewer avoid answering the question. At the same time, the interviewee should be encouraged to continue with his report. This can best be achieved by restating the implied meaning of the question and redirecting the revised question back to the interviewee. For example, the interviewee asked, "Did the principal think the teacher lied about me?" The interviewer responded with "You mean it wasn't clear whether the teacher lied or not?" "Right," replied the interviewee, "You remember when . . ."

7. When interviewee contradictions arise, the interviewer can quote the interviewee, but he must be careful not to antagonize him. One good device is for the interviewer to restate the earlier remark with something like the following: "I want to be sure to get this right, and I wonder if I haven't made a mistake. Would you please clarify your last statement in light

of your earlier comment?" If this is enough, fine. However, in most cases, the interviewer will have to restate the previous statement before the interviewee will respond.

8. When the interviewee digresses, the interviewer can lead the interviewee back to relevant material by questions which relate to what he has been saying about the topic.

9. When the interviewer wants to elicit additional information from the interviewee or clarify information already given, a number of probing techniques may be used. They enable the interviewer to bring about a reaction without himself becoming part of the reaction. Thus, to elicit additional information the interviewer uses such phrases as "Would you tell me some more about that?", "I'm interested in what you're saying. Could you give me a little more information about it?", or "I see what you mean. Can you tell me a little bit more about how you feel?" These statements indicate that the interviewer is interested, understands what the interviewee is saying, and is making a direct bid for more information.

Let's consider some examples of probes for additional information within an actual interviewing situation.

Interviewer: How do you feel about federal aid to ghettos?

Interviewee: Well, I don't know. Sometimes I think we go too far.

Interviewer: I see. Can you tell me a little more about what you have in mind?

Interviewee: Maybe we ought to give some help. But gosh, when I see tax money going to help someone who refuses to help himself or even demonstrates against the United States, I think we'd better lay off.

Interviewer: Sometimes you feel we ought not to help them?

Interviewee: That's right! I think they're lazy, irresponsible, and no good.

In this example, the interviewee made a mildly critical statement at first. The interviewer reacted to this by being nonevaluative and yet accepting. He didn't criticize the interviewee nor did he agree with him; he merely indicated a general acceptance of the statement. The result of this was a somewhat more critical statement. The nonevaluative acceptance by the interviewer permitted the interviewee to make his final, bitter response without feeling the need to defend or modify it.

Another type of eliciting probe is the inflection of emphasis. For example, if the interviewer's question has a slight rising inflection on the end, indicating a mild "I don't quite get you" connotation, the interviewee will usually respond with additional information to clarify his point.

Another type of eliciting probe is the direct bid for additional information. Here the stress is put on words such as "Kinds" in that it asks the interviewee to shift from his present frame of reference to other "Kinds" of things about which the interviewer is interested.

To clarify information already given, the interviewer might use such probes as "Now let me see if I have it straight. As I understand it, you feel . . .," and then summarize what the interviewee has said.

Let's consider an example of probes for clarifying information already given.

Interviewer: If I remember correctly, you said that last quarter was a particularly bad quarter for you as far as absences were concerned. How many times were you absent last quarter?

Interviewee: Well, with the school play and the traveling assembly, I'd say I missed about five or six times.

Interviewer: I see. Five or six times? Can you give me a little closer estimate?

Interviewee: Well, like I said, there were an awful lot of school activities, but I guess I missed a few more times than five or six.

Interviewer: Pause.

Interviewee: Probably between ten and twelve times to be more exact.

Interviewer: Ten or twelve you say. Which would be the most accurate?

Interviewee: Oh, I think twelve would probably be more like it.

Notice that the interviewer referred back to some incomplete information by repeating the interviewee's earlier statement with the added emphasis that he was interested in having the interviewee explain more about it. The interviewee readily responded to the interviewer's statement. Then after the interviewee's first estimate, the interviewer began with a non-evaluative statement by merely repeating the interviewee's first estimate. It seems apparent that his first response was

more concerned with the reasons why he had been absent.
When the interviewer ignored the reasons why and focused
on the factual part of the response, the interviewee responded
with more accurate information.

10. Finally, if the interviewee shows resistance, the interviewer
should merely ask the interviewee to talk about it. In response, the interviewee will usually mention a problem or
problem area which in itself resolves the interviewer's immediate problem — resistance. However, often there is a
deeper reason why the interviewee fails to understand the
question or gives an answer which does not actually answer
the question, namely, the question arouses anxiety in him.
The interviewer must learn to detect signs of anxiety, and
must judge when it is wisest to stop the line of questioning
even if he has not obtained the information the objectives
called for. A further danger is the fact that the interviewer
himself may feel anxious about a problem and may therefore
be oversensitive to signs of disturbance in the interviewee.

11. The interviewer should know when to end the interview. For
example, if all of the purposes have been satisfactorily met,
then stop. However, most of the time, problems will be encountered that weren't anticipated. The suggested procedure
here is to probe until the interviewer feels that to probe
further would jeopardize the successful completion of the
interview. At this point, the interviewer should encourage a
break in the interview. There should be an understanding that
to continue without further information or thought would not
lead to the purposes they had agreed on at the beginning of the
interview. And if possible, get some purposes for the interim
period so that the interviewer and interviewee would be prepared to start where they left off.

A Value Model: A Programmed Text

G. GARY CASPER

To aid in teaching the procedures presented in Chapter 3, a self-instruction programmed text was written. The terminology, basic structure, and use of the simple value model described in Chapter 3 is presented. Once the simple model is thoroughly understood and mastered, one can then proceed to learn and use the more comprehensive Extended Procedure described in Chapter 3.

The text was developed and at least partially validated with high school sophomores and can therefore be used at that level, or above. It is important to note that the programmed text was developed and validated with students who had never been otherwise introduced to the material in Chapter 3.

To permit adequate time for students to work through the programmed text, it is suggested that a full 5-day week of 50-minute class periods be allocated to its use. This time should prove to be more than adequate since the development and validation experiences indicate maximum student completion time of approximately 3 hours. Students finishing early could use the extra time for consultation with the teacher in selection of topics, or in related areas.

Two possibilities for introducing the programmed text into the classroom appear to have promise. One would suggest that the text be presented with little or no introduction, and then be followed by working through several short issues, utilizing the simple model. However, the author favors a second approach which would have the students first introduced to the simple model by the teacher, and then led through an example of the use of the model. The text would next be presented and upon its completion more extensive practice in the use of the model could be implemented. Obviously, the above-mentioned approaches are not exhaustive of the possibilities, and the teacher is free to experiment with other approaches in introducing the text at an appropriate time.

Regardless of the manner in which the text is first presented, it is suggested that it can be followed with extensive practice in joint efforts with the teacher working through several examples of its use. Thus, the terminology and model learned from the text can be integrated in using the simple model. Then, introduction of the Extended Procedure readily follows with the student in possession of the necessary skills with which to learn effective use of the tool.

LESSON I

RATINGS & DESCRIPTIONS

Objective: To teach the terms: *rating, value object, value term, description* and *feature*.

To teach discrimination between *ratings* and *descriptions*.

I-1. What is a *rating?*
These are ratings. Look them over.
   a. Stage scenery is good.
   b. The storage cabinets are satisfactory.
   c. P.A. lockers seem sufficient.
   d. The props were ample.
   e. That paper cutter is dependable.

BUT, the following statements are NOT ratings. They are descriptions. YOU find the difference between these *descriptions* and the *ratings* above.
   a. The "107" is a photocopier.
   b. Those iron filings are magnetized.
   c. Wet-mounts are glued.
   d. His room has acoustical tile.

Question #I-1:
Let's see if you discovered the clues to recognize *ratings*. Of the following statements, *two* are ratings. Underline the two ratings.
   a. A tack-iron is electric.
   b. Enlarging is desirable.
   c. Overhead projectors are good.
   d. The dry-press was chromed.

Answer to question #I-1:
   b. Enlarging is desirable.
   c. Overhead projectors are good.

I-2. A rating makes a value judgment about something. Did you discover this? Look at these examples:

   a. The tickets are excellent. (rating)

   b. The tickets are cardboard. (description)

Sentence *a* is a rating because the word "excellent" is a value judgment about the tickets. In some manner, the tickets have been judged excellent.

Sentence *b* is NOT a rating but a description because the word cardboard makes a factual statement about the tickets instead of a judgment.

   c. A yearbook is beneficial. (rating)

   d. A yearbook is lithographed. (description)

Sentence *c* is a rating because the word beneficial makes the statement into a value judgment about the yearbook.

Sentence *d* is a description, NOT a rating, because the word *lithographed* makes the sentence into a factual statement about the yearbook. It is NOT a value judgment but a description.

New Idea.

A *rating* has two parts: (1) the *value object* and (2) the *value term*.

Study these examples:

   a. Rating — value object / value term
              Microphones   are good.

   b. Rating — value object / value term
              The lighting   is satisfactory.

   c. Rating — value object / value term
              Transistors   are worthwhile.

Question #I-2:

Work these for practice. Label the two parts of the rating by putting *value object* and *value term* above the correct part. Use the above examples as models.

   a. ‾‾‾‾‾‾‾‾‾‾
      The stage plan   /   ‾‾‾‾‾‾‾
                                is efficient.

   b. ‾‾‾‾‾‾‾‾‾‾
      Three light bars   /   ‾‾‾‾‾‾‾
                                are accurate.

   c. ‾‾‾‾‾‾‾‾‾‾‾‾
      That mimeo machine   /   ‾‾‾‾‾‾‾‾
                                seems dependable.

Answer to question #I-2:

   The first column are all *value objects* and the second column are all *value terms*.

I-3. Thus a *rating* contains a value term such as in these examples:
   a. A signal is reliable.
   b. The orchestra is capable.
   c. Those signatures are excellent.

Question #I-3:
Label the value objects and value terms in each of the above ratings.

Answer to question #I-3:

value object	value term
a. A signal	reliable
b. The orchestra	capable
c. Those signatures	excellent

Question #I-4:
Two of the following sentences are ratings. Underline the ratings, and label the value objects and value terms.
   a. The microphones are fine.
   b. A floor plug is metal.
   c. Boom-stands are acceptable.
   d. A co-axial cable has nine channels.

Answer to question #I-4:

value object	value term
a. The microphones	fine
c. Boom-stands	acceptable

I-5. A *description* typically makes a factual statement about the value object. That is, a *description* describes the value object in terms of some property, attribute or feature it possesses.
   a. The record cloth was anti-static.
   b. A Xetron lamp is 1500 watts.
   c. The Ampex tape recorders are stereo-channeled.

Question #I-5:
Of the three statements below, which are *descriptions?* Underline the answer.
   a. The Bridge is the master control.
   b. The first recording was fine.
   c. The Air Force film is black and white.

Answer to question #I-5:
   a. The Bridge is the master control.
   c. The Air Force film is black and white.

I-6. A *description* contains two parts: (1) the *value object* and (2) the *characteristic*. Recall that the value object is that item which you speak about. A characteristic is some feature, property or attribute of the value object.

Examples of descriptions:

a. Description: <u>value object</u> / <u>characteristic</u>
The remote band   is 30 watts.

b. Description: <u>value object</u> / <u>characteristic</u>
The connection   is an alligator clip.

Question #I-6:
Label the *parts* of these descriptions.

a. Description: —————— / ——————
The tone arm   is a Dual.

b. Description: —————— / ——————
Your tape   is red oxide.

c. Description: —————— / ——————
That power load   was 3,500 watts.

d. Description: —————— / ——————
Silicone   is the lubricant.

Answer to question #I-6:

a. Description: <u>value object</u> / <u>characteristic</u>
The tone arm   is a Dual.

b. Description: <u>value object</u> / <u>characteristic</u>
Your tape   is red oxide.

c. Description: <u>value object</u> / <u>characteristic</u>
That power load   was 3,500 watts.

d. Description: <u>value object</u> / <u>characteristic</u>
Silicone   is the lubricant.

I-7. NOTE WHAT THE *DIFFERENCES* ARE BETWEEN A *RATING* AND A *DESCRIPTION*. Earlier you learned that a rating has two parts: (1) a *value object*, and (2) a *value term* as in this example:

Rating: <u>value object</u> / <u>value term</u>
The frost gel   is good.

A description has two parts also: (1) a *value object*, and (2) a *characteristic*:

Description: <u>value object</u> / <u>characteristic</u>
The headset   is volume powered.

Question #I-7:
The two parts of a rating are the ————————— and the

————————— .

Answer to question #I-7:
The two parts of a rating are the *value object* and the *value term*.

I-8. Name the two parts of a description in order.
A Description has a _____ and a _____ .

Answer to question #I-8 :
Description = <u>value object</u> / <u>characteristic</u>

Question #I-9:
Identify these statements by writing *Rating* or by writing *Description* in the blanks as needed. Use the above examples as a review if desired.

_____ a. The high hat spots are 500 watt lamps.
_____ b. A baby spot is nice.
_____ c. The 14th Amendment abolished slavery.
_____ d. Three inputs were good.

Answer to question #I-9:

<u>Description</u>   a. The high hat spots are 500 watt lamps.
<u>Rating</u>   b. A baby spot is nice.
<u>Description</u>   c. The 14th Amendment abolished slavery.
<u>Rating</u>   d. Three inputs were good.

Question #I-10:
Identify the following examples as *ratings* or *descriptions* **and** label the parts as has been done in example a.

		value object	/	characteristic
<u>Description</u>	a.	The column lights		are red floods.
_____	b.	Scene A uses blue lights.		
_____	c.	Taxation without representation elicited the Revolutionary War.		
_____	d.	The magenta flood is satisfactory.		
_____	e.	Orchestra lights are splendid.		
_____	f.	Ceiling lamps are reds and surprise pink floods.		
_____	g.	The catwalk is pleasant.		

Answer to question #I-10:

<u>Description</u>	a.	<u>value object</u> The column lights	/	<u>characteristic</u> are red floods.
<u>Description</u>	b.	<u>value object</u> Scene A	/	<u>characteristic</u> uses blue lights.
<u>Description</u>	c.	<u>value object</u> Taxation without representation	/	<u>characteristic</u> elicited the Revolutionary War.

Rating _____	d.	$\dfrac{\text{value object}}{\text{The magenta flood}}$	/	$\dfrac{\text{value term}}{\text{is satisfactory.}}$
Rating _____	e.	$\dfrac{\text{value object}}{\text{Orchestra lights}}$	/	$\dfrac{\text{value term}}{\text{are splendid.}}$
Description _____	f.	$\dfrac{\text{value object}}{\text{Ceiling lamps}}$	/	$\dfrac{\text{characteristic}}{\text{are reds and surprise pink floods.}}$
Rating _____	g.	$\dfrac{\text{value object}}{\text{The catwalk}}$	/	$\dfrac{\text{value term}}{\text{is pleasant.}}$

SUMMARY

In this lesson, the terms *rating, value object, value term, description,* and *characteristic* were introduced.

You learned that a rating contains two parts: a value object, that which you evaluate; and a value term, some kind of value judgment concerning the value object. For example:

Rating: $\dfrac{\text{value object}}{\text{Ice Cream}}$ / $\dfrac{\text{value term}}{\text{is good.}}$

A description typically makes a factual statement about the value object. Thus a description contains two parts, the value object and a characteristic. For example:

Description: $\dfrac{\text{value object}}{\text{The ceiling beams}}$ / $\dfrac{\text{characteristic}}{\text{are at a 45 degree angle.}}$

The difference between a rating and a description was examined and examples were given to identify both types of statements.

You should now be able to recognize ratings and descriptions and to write examples of your own.

If you need to stop for any reason, this would be a good spot. Otherwise, PROCEED TO LESSON II.

LESSON II

CRITERION

Objective: To teach recognition of *criterion*.
   To give practice in discriminating among *ratings, descriptions,* and *criteria.*

II-1. This is a *criterion*:
   CRITERION: Lamps which are double-weight are good.
And this:
   CRITERION: Films which have three reels are interesting.
   We speak of one *criterion*, but we speak of two or more *criteria.* Criteria then is the plural of criterion.

Question #II-1:
Two of these four sentences are criterion statements (criteria). Underline each criterion. Do nothing to the other sentences.
    a. A record which is band one is superb.
    b. An auditorium dubbing is fine.
    c. The green filter was glass.
    d. An outlet which is three-way is reliable.

Answer to question #II-1:
    a. <u>A record which is band one is superb.</u>
    d. <u>An outlet which is three-way is reliable.</u>

II-2. A *criterion* contains both the idea of *rating* and of a *description*. Note how this is achieved.
Example a:
    Rating: Red flood lamps are good.
    Description: Red flood lamps are double-weight.
    Criterion: Lights which are double-weight are good.
Example b:
    Rating: The rehearsal groups are acceptable.
    Description: The rehearsal groups are troupers.
    Criterion: People who are troupers are acceptable.
Question #II-2:
    Write the criterion for the following:
    Rating: A hexagon screwdriver is useful.
    Description: A hexagon screwdriver is magnetized.
    Criterion: A screwdriver _____ .

Answer to question #II-2:
    Criterion: A screwdriver which is magnetized is useful.

II-3. A *criterion* is composed of three items:
    Comparison class, characteristic, and *value term.*
    In a criterion, the *characteristic* comes from the *description*; the *value term* comes from the *rating*.

The inter-relations of the rating and description are critical if they are to form a meaningful criterion. The description must be relevant to the value judgment reflected in the rating. For example, if one were thinking of carrying groceries in a paper bag, he might say that "Paper bags are useful," which is a rating. It would then seem logically odd to select the description that "Paper bags burn" since this description is not really related to the original point-of-view regarding carrying groceries. A much more applicable description would seem to be, "Paper bags are light in weight," since this description relates directly to the usefulness of paper bags in carrying groceries. It is vital that you keep in mind the necessity for this inter-relatedness between the rating and description. More will be said about this later when we investigate points-of-view. Below are examples of criterion statements:

comparison class /	characteristic /	value term
a. Foods	which contain sugar	are good.

comparison class /	characteristic /	value term
b. Persons	who are trained	are better.

comparison class /	characteristic /	value term
c. Timers	which show seconds	are invaluable.

Question #II-3:

Label the three parts of each criterion below:

_____ /	_____ /	_____
a. Wiring	which has slide bars	is dependable.

_____ /	_____ /	_____
b. Copiers	which are single units	are best.

_____ /	_____ /	_____
c. Signals	which are electronic	seem poor.

Answer to question #II-3:

comparison class /	characteristic /	value term
a. Wiring	which has slide bars	is dependable.

comparison class /	characteristic /	value term
b. Copiers	which are single units	are best.

comparison class /	characteristic /	value term
c. Signals	which are electronic	seem poor.

Question #II-4:

Complete each criterion below. Fill in the words which serve as the *characteristic* and as the *value term*.

Set a.

      Rating: Plastic tape is satisfactory.
      Description: Plastic tape is an insulator.
      Criterion: Material which _____.

Set b.

      Rating: Imprinted circuitry is reliable.
      Description: Imprinted circuitry is in some T.V. sets.
      Criterion: Wiring which _____.

Set c.

      Rating: The blackboard is efficient.
      Description: The blackboard is moveable.
      Criterion: A writing-surface _____.

Answer to question #II-4:

Set a.

   Criterion: Material which is an insulator is satisfactory.

Set b.

   Criterion: Wiring which is in some T.V. sets is reliable.

Set c.

   Criterion: A writing-surface which is moveable is efficient.

II-5. In each of the previous examples, a comparison class was provided. It is now important that you understand the idea of *comparison class*. Therefore, examine the different parts *ratings* and *descriptions* have as contrasted to *criteria*.

First: Ratings and descriptions have a value object which is a *specific* item, group or class.

Second: Criteria have a comparison class which always refers to a more general group or class.

Stated in another manner: The *value object* is a *specific* item.

           The *comparison class* is a more *general group* to which the value object belongs.

Examples:

  Rating: The RCA projector is adequate.

(The value object is *The RCA projector* which is a *specific* item.)

  Description: The RCA projector is two speed.

(The value object is *The RCA projector* which is a *specific* item.)

  Criterion: A machine which is two speed is adequate.

(The comparison class is *machine* which is more *general* including not only RCA, but Bell & Howell, Kodak, etc.)

 In Summary, then, a *value object* refers to a *specific* item, group or class while a *comparison class* refers to a more general group or class.

Question #II-5:

Use examples *a* and *b* shown below to fill in the blanks.

Example a:

   Rating: Boeing 707 Jets are suitable.

   Description: Boeing 707 Jets are fast.

   Criterion: Airliners which are fast are suitable.

Example b:

   Rating: 3M copy-paper is good.

   Description: 3M copy-paper is watermarked.

   Criterion: Copy-paper which is watermarked is good.

1. In example *a*, the specific item is _____ and the comparison class is _____ .

2. In example *b*, the specific item is _____ and the comparison class is _____ .

Answer to question #II-5:

1. In example *a*, the specific item is *Boeing 707 Jets* and the comparison class is *Airliners*.
2. In example *b*, the specific item is *3M copy-paper* and the comparison class is *copy-paper*.

Question #II-6:

In the two sets below, identify the underlined words in two ways by (1) writing *specific* or *general* in Column A, and (2) put the correct name (either value object or comparison class) of the underlined part in Column B. The first one has been done as an example.

Column A   *Column B*

specific   Rating: <u>NASA demonstrations</u>   value object
                        are ideal.

_____ Description: <u>NASA demonstrations</u>   _____
                        use films.

_____ Criterion: <u>Programs</u> which use   _____
                        films are excellent.

_____ Rating: <u>A ground-adapter</u>   _____
                        is useful.

_____ Description: <u>A ground-adapter</u>   _____
                        bridges the power.

_____ Criterion: <u>A device</u> which bridges   _____
                        the power is useful.

Answer to question #II-6:

Column A   *Column B*

specific   Rating: <u>NASA demonstrations</u>   value object
                        are ideal.

specific   Description: <u>NASA demonstrations</u>   value object
                        use films.

general   Criterion: <u>Programs</u> which use   comparison class
                        films are excellent.

specific   Rating: <u>A ground-adapter</u>   value object
                        is useful.

specific   Description: <u>A ground-adapter</u>   value object
                        bridges the power.

general   Criterion: <u>A device</u> which bridges   comparison class
                        the power is useful.

Question #II-7 (Review):

Identify these statements by putting *rating, description,* or *criterion* in the blanks.

Set a.

_____ Film Leader is flexible.

_____ Plastic which is flexible is good.

_____ Film Leader is good.

Set b.

_____ Devices which are heat proof are excellent.

_____ Stop-action shutters are excellent.

_____ Stop-action shutters are heat proof.

Set c.

_____ One-minute commercials are interesting.

_____ Films which are concise are interesting.

_____ One-minute commercials are concise.

Answer to question #II-7:

Set a.

Description   Film leader is flexible.

Criterion   Plastic which is flexible is good.

Rating   Film leader is good.

Set b.

Criterion   Devices which are heat proof are excellent.

Rating   Stop-action shutters are excellent.

Description   Stop-action shutters are heat proof.

Set c.

Rating   One-minute commercials are interesting.

Criterion   Films which are corcise are interesting.

Description   One-minute commercials are concise.

II-8. Now that you know the parts of a criterion, you should notice that the parts may not always be in the same order. Up to now the parts have been presented in the order of comparison class, characteristic and value term. It is possible to shift these around. For example:

    a. Clothing which is warm is good.

    b. Warm clothing is good.

    c. Good clothing is warm.

All of the above reflect the same criterion although the statements differ. Notice that example (b) looks suspiciously like a rating and example (c) like a description. However, in this case they are criterion statements because the comparison class of concern is clothing rather than the value objects "warm clothing" or "good clothing." Therefore, to know if a statement is a criterion it is very important to know if you have a general comparison class or whether you are dealing with a specific item, i.e., a value object. This is determined from the context of the discussion in which you are engaged.

SUMMARY

Recognition of *criteria* was the principal goal of LESSON II. A criterion contains the idea of a rating, of a description, and a comparison class. A criterion contains three parts: a *comparison class*, a *characteristic* and a *value term*.

In a criterion, the characteristic comes from a description; the value term comes from a rating. Together they give validity to a criterion.

A good deal more will be said about comparison classes later, but for now you have learned that ratings and descriptions deal with *specific* items, groups or classes as the *value object*. But, a criterion refers to a more *general group* or class as its *comparison class*.

Should you need to stop, this would be an opportune time. If not, PROCEED TO LESSON III.

LESSON III

RANKING AND GRADING

Objective: To teach the concepts *ranking* and *grading*.
   To teach discriminations between *ranking* and *grading*.

Question #III-1:
Suppose you were asked to rank the following five numbers from the lowest to highest: 9, 3, 6, 4, 1. How would you do it?

Answer to question #III-1:
   1, 3, 4, 6, 9.

III-2. Among the important things you did to answer the question was to recognize that the request to rank the numbers required you to order them in some way. It is the process by which you ordered these numbers that is necessary to understand ranking.

To accomplish the task you probably compared the numbers saying, 3 is greater than 1, 4 is greater than 3 etc. and wrote down the answer.

Question #III-2:
Suppose you went to the store and found that you could purchase some green apples at 10 cents a pound, red apples at 5 cents a pound and yellow apples at 20 cents a pound. Since you want the most pounds for your money, rank the apples from least expensive to most expensive.

Answer to question #III-2:
Red apples, green apples and yellow apples.

Question #III-3:
Upon what basis were the apples ranked?

Answer to question #III-3:
Upon the basis of cost from least expensive to most expensive.

Question #III-4:
In what way other than cost might they have been ranked?

Answer to question #III-4:
Taste, shape, size, beauty, color, etc.

III-5. I might have stated my basis as follows:
          Apples which cost least are best.

Question #III-5:
What kind of a statement is this?

Answer to question #III-5:
A criterion statement.

Question #III-6:
In the criterion, "Apples which cost least are best," what is the comparison class, characteristic and value term?

Answer to question #III-6:

Comparison class	/	characteristic	/	value term
Apples		which cost least		are best.

III-7. Now, suppose we change our basis of comparison from cost to taste and you are given a new criterion:
          Red apples taste best.

Question #III-7:
On the basis of this criterion, could you now rank the green, red and yellow apples?

Answer to question #III-7:
No. If you are in doubt about this answer, the following frames should clear up your confusion.

III-8. The criterion tells me only that red apples taste best. This tells me only that red apples taste better than either the green apples or yellow apples.

Question #III-8:
What else do you suppose I need to know?

Answer to question #III-8:
Whether green apples taste better than yellow apples, or yellow apples taste better than green apples.

Question #III-9:
Therefore, I need another_____ statement.

Answer to question #III-9:
Criterion.

Question #III-10:
What do you think the criterion statement should say? Hint: The first criterion was about the apples that taste best. Make this criterion about the apples that taste worst.

Answer to question #III-10:
It might read that "Yellow apples taste the worst," or that "Green apples taste the worst."

Question #III-11:
Given the following criteria:
    a. Red apples taste best.
    b. Yellow apples taste worst.
Rank the following: green apples, red apples, and yellow apples.

Answer to question #III-11:
    a. Red apples
    b. Green apples
    c. Yellow apples

III-12. In the preceding examples you were asked to "rank" the apples based upon taste. This you accomplished by comparing each apple to the other and deciding which apple was better than the other according to the criteria being used to describe better than.
The process of evaluating an object in comparative terms such as better than, worse than, or the same as another object is called *ranking*.

Question #III-12:
The distinguishing characteristic of a ranking process is the decision that an object is _____ , _____ , or _____ another object.

Answer to question #III-12:
   The same as, worse than, or better than.

III-13. Now that you have learned how to evaluate with rankings
   there is another evaluative process with which we are concerned. It is called *grading*.
   The evaluative process of grading requires a decision as
   to whether a value object belongs to some category or not.
   The example of the green, red and yellow apples provides
   three distinct categories based upon color. Grading would
   then involve decisions as to whether an apple belonged to
   one of these categories or not.

Question #III-13:
   Suppose you purchased an apple at the store. To grade it into one
   of the three categories (red, green, or yellow apples), you would
   only need to look at its _____ .

Answer to question #III-13:
   Color.

III-14. As a matter of fact, sometimes the categories are themselves referred to as grades as occurs with milk: Grade AA
   or Grade A milk. Other names used are homogenized,
   pasteurized and raw milk, each of which is a separate category. Given some milk, a grading would be required to
   decide which name to apply to that milk.

Question #III-14:
   By now you should understand that grading involves a decision
   of whether or not a value object belongs to some _____ .

Answer to question #III-14:
   Category.

III-15. The following ratings also involve gradings. Look them over!
   a. Being unemployed is bad.
   b. Having a job is good.
   c. Going to school is good.
   d. Going to jail is bad.

Question #III-15:
   We already know the parts of a rating are the _____
   and the _____ .

Answer to question #III-15:
   Value object and value term.

Question #III-16:
   In each of these ratings the value term is what?

Answer to question #III-16:
Either the term good or the term bad.

Question #III-17:
Therefore, you might decide that a grading in these examples involves evaluating a value object as either in the category_____ or the category_____ .

Answer to question #III-17:
Good or bad.

Question #III-18:
If your answer agrees with the one given, either the category good or the category bad, you are beginning to understand what a grading is. Look at the following examples and identify the gradings as well as the rankings.

    a. Murder is bad.
    b. Shooting someone is better than being shot.
    c. Mother's apple pie is better than store pie.
    d. Mother's pie is good.

Answer to question #III-18:
    a. grading
    b. ranking
    c. ranking
    d. grading

III-19. If you missed items *a* or *d* reread the above discussion on grading. If you missed items *b* or *c* return to the section on ranking. If your answer agrees, good for you! You have learned that ranking involves choices of better than, worse than or same as and that gradings involve choices of whether the value object belongs to a given category or not.

The following examples are gradings that use value terms other than good or bad.

    a. Junk is worthless.
    b. Music is desirable.
    c. Illness is undesirable.
    d. Piano lessons are worthwhile.

Question #III-19:
What new value terms have been introduced?

Answer to question #III-19:
Worthless, desirable, undesirable, worthwhile.

Question #III-20:
Can you pair these value terms into opposites as in good and bad?
Do so.

Answer to question #III-20:
Yes. Desirable — undesirable, worthwhile — worthless.

Question #III-21:
Therefore, you can now say that gradings involve evaluating
whether a value object belongs to a given category or not such as
good or bad, _____ or _____ , and
_____ or _____ .

Answer to question #III-21:
Desirable or undesirable, worthwhile or worthless (or vice versa).

SUMMARY

It should now be reasonable to say a grading involves an evaluation that a value object either belongs to a category or not. In
contrast, a ranking is concerned with a comparison such as better
than, worse than or same as.

Another way of viewing a grading is to think in terms of evaluating the value object itself against the chosen criteria to decide
if it belongs in some category.

GRADING

	evaluated by	category or	good-bad
Value object —	description and criteria	— value term	— desirable-undesirable worthwhile-worthless

Contrast this with a ranking which would appear as:

RANKING

Value object & another object —	compared & evaluated by criteria	— value term —	better than the same as worse than

This is a good breaking point if you must stop for a while. If
not, PROCEED TO LESSON IV.

LESSON IV

LOGIC AND PRINCIPLES

Objective: To illustrate the *logical* nature of the Value-Decision
Model.
To teach the meaning of a *principle*.

IV-1. The classical example of deductive logic is the syllogism. It
possesses three parts:
   a. A major premise
   b. A minor premise
   c. A conclusion
An example is as follows:

a. Vehicles with two wheels are called bicycles.   (Major premise)
b. My vehicle has two wheels.   (Minor premise)
c. Therefore, my vehicle is a bicycle.   (Conclusion)

Notice that none of the statements in the example syllogism contain value terms. However, it is easily seen that a syllogism containing value terms could be constructed. For example:

a. Toys with sharp points are bad.   (Major premise)
b. My toy has sharp points.   (Minor premise)
c. Therefore, my toy is bad.   (Conclusion)

Suppose now that the three types of statements in the Value-
Decision Model (the rating, description and criterion) could be
fitted into the form of a syllogism. If this were true, then the
properties of deductive logic would apply to the Value-Decision
Model. Let's now investigate this possibility.

Question #IV-1:
What name have you learned for statements like the one in *a* of
the last example above?

Answer to question #IV-1:
A criterion. If you didn't answer criterion, look at *a* again closely.

Question #IV-2:
What name have you learned for statements like the one in *b*
above?

Answer to question #IV-2:
A description. Again, if you made a mistake look *b* over again.

Question #IV-3:
What kind of statement do you suppose *c* is?

Answer to question #IV-3:
If you say a rating, you're right.

IV-4. Therefore, the Value-Decision Model you are learning is in the truest sense *a logical model* with its parts representing a syllogism as follows:
    a. major premise — a criterion
    b. minor premise — a description
    c. conclusion   — a rating

Question #IV-4:
    Complete the following syllogism:
    a. Black houses are ugly.
    b. _____ .
    c. Therefore, your house is ugly.

Answer to question #IV-4:
    b. Your house is black.

Question #IV-5:
Referring back to the information in IV-4, notice that a syllogism has three parts and that these parts correspond to the three parts of the Value-Decision Model.

Therefore, we can say that the statement "Black houses are ugly" is the a. _____ of the syllogism and the b. _____ of the Value-Decision Model. "Your house is black" is the c. _____ part of the syllogism and the d. _____ of the Value-Decision Model while "Therefore, your house is ugly" is the e. _____ of the syllogism and the f. _____ of the Value-Decision Model.

Answer to question #IV-5:
    a. Major premise   b. Criterion
    c. Minor premise   d. Description
    e. Conclusion   f. Rating

IV-6. The rating is a conclusion for which we offer the criterion and description as support. *This is the essence of the evaluation process.* Suppose I state that "Your house is ugly." You have every reason to expect that I have some basis of support for such a statement and so you ask, "Why would you say that?"

Question #IV-6:
You would expect me to offer the above _____ and _____ in support of my rating.

Answer to question #IV-6:
Criterion and description.

Question #IV-7:
Since it contains all the parts of the syllogism, we can say the Value-Decision Model is a log_ _ _ _l model with a major premise,

the _____ , and a minor premise, the _____ , and the conclusion, a _____ .

Answer to question #IV-7:
  Logical model
  Major premise — criterion
  Minor premise — description
  Conclusion   — rating

Question #IV-8:
  Therefore, the criterion and description are offered as _____ for the conclusion, the rating.

Answer to question #IV-8:
  Support.

Question #IV-9:
  This is why we can say the Value-Decision Model is a _____ model.

Answer to question #IV-9:
  Logical model.

IV-10. Now, if a criterion and a description offer support for a conclusion (rating), how much better off we would be if we could present two criteria and description combinations in support of our conclusion. Or three! Or four!

Question #IV-10:
  Other things being equal, wouldn't you be more inclined to accept a conclusion supported by multiple criteria and description combinations rather than a single one?

Answer to question #IV-10:
  I'm sure you said yes to this question.

IV-11. Look at the following diagram:

Example 1

Rating
|
Description
Criterion

Example 2

Rating

Description   Description
Criterion   Criterion

Example 3

Rating

Description   Description   Description
Criterion   Criterion   Criterion

Question #IV-11:
Which of the above examples looks most stable to you and thus least likely to be toppled?

Answer to question #IV-11:
Obviously, example 3 with the widest base or, in other words, with the most support is the most stable.

IV-12. Ratings supported by more than one set of a description and a criterion are said to reflect a "principle." The principle thus contains the several characteristics derived from the criteria. It is the multiple characteristics that identify the principle as opposed to a criterion which contains but one characteristic.

Question #IV-12:
Therefore, more than one criterion offered in support of a rating is called a _____ .

Answer to question #IV-12:
Principle.

IV-13. Notice that a principle requires a combination of characteristics from the applicable criteria. In other words, the principle reflects the several characteristics contained in the criteria.

Question #IV-13:
When a rating is supported by only one description and a criterion, we speak of the support as a criterion; but when more than one criteria are offered, we speak of a _____ .

Answer to question #IV-13:
Principle.

Question #IV-14:
In your own words, what is a principle?

Answer to question #IV-14:
Your answer must reflect the fact that a principle has several characteristics derived from two or more criteria.

Question #IV-15:
We may, therefore, speak of the Value-Decision Model as a a. _____ model in which the conclusion is a b. _____ supported by a major premise, a c. _____ , and by a minor premise, a d. _____ . Further, if more than one criteria is offered, we speak of a e. _____ .

Answer to question #IV-15:
a. logical, b. rating, c. criterion, d. description, e. principle.

Question #IV-16:

Was your answer correct? If your answer is no, write no in the space provided and return to the beginning of Lesson IV. If your answer is yes, go on.

Put your answer here _____ .

SUMMARY

You just learned that the Value-Decision Model is a logical model where the *major premise, minor premise* and *conclusion* of a syllogism are represented by the *criterion, description* and *rating* respectively.

Further, you learned that a rating can be supported by a single set of criterion and a description. However, if more than one set is offered in support of a rating, it becomes more easily accepted since the support is greater.

When more than one set of a description and criterion are offered in support of a rating, the several characteristics described in the criteria define a principle. In other words, a principle has several characteristics derived from two or more criteria.

Should you need to stop, this is a good spot. If not, PROCEED TO LESSON V.

LESSON V

PRINCIPLE STATEMENTS

Objectives: To define a *principle statement.*

To establish a procedure for writing principle statements.

V-1. In Lesson IV you learned that the Value-Decision Model is a logical model in which a rating is supported by a criterion and description. When there is a combination of more than one criteria, the combination is termed a principle.

The idea was presented that a principle offered more stable and reliable support, other things being equal, than a single criterion could.

Question #V-1:

Define, in your own words, a principle.

Answer to question #V-1:

The answer should reflect the fact that a principle is established by two or more criteria from which several characteristics can be derived.

V-2. The problem now arises as to how a principle might be stated. An example might give a clue.

    Rating: John's car is good.

    Criterion 1: Cars that run are good.

    Description 1: John's car runs.

    Criterion 2: Cars that go 100 mph are good.

    Description 2: John's car goes 100 mph.

Question #V-2:

Since two criteria are listed, a _____ is represented.

Answer to question #V-2:

Principle.

Question #V-3:

By listing each of the _____ , we have described the

_____ .

Answer to question #V-3:

Criteria, principle.

V-4. Look at the following statements:

    a. Cars that are 1970 models and cost more than $3,000, are good.

    b. Cars that are American made and use regular gas, are good.

    c. Cars that get 17 miles per gallon of gas and use no oil, are good.

Question #V-4:

What kind of statements do they appear to be?

Answer to question #V-4:

Criterion statements. You might also have noticed that they are statements of principle, i.e., they have more than one characteristic.

Question #V-5:

How many characteristics does each have?

Answer to question #V-5:

Each has two characteristics.

Question #V-6:

See if you can write such a principle statement combining the two criteria in item V-2.

Answer to question #V-6:
Your answer should look something like this:
Cars that run and go 100 mph are good.

V-7. You have just written a *principle statement*. Of course it's
not a very elaborate one, but consider the benefits of such a
statement where many criteria can be combined into a single
statement. Notice that the descriptions applicable to the principle are implied by the characteristics they provide to the
criteria. Thus to write a principle statement we need only
refer to the criteria.

Question #V-7:
By definition then, several criteria, or in other words, a principle,
can be combined into a single_____ _____.

Answer to question #V-7:
Principle statement.

Question #V-8:
Given the following criteria:
    a. Blue cars are best.
    b. Convertible cars are best.
    c. Cars with bucket seats are best.
What is the comparison class?

Answer to question #V-8:
Cars is the comparison class.

Question #V-9:
How many characteristics are represented?

Answer to question #V-9:
Three. Blue, convertible, and bucket seats.

Question #V-10:
What value terms are present?

Answer to question #V-10:
Only one, the value term best.

Question #V-11:
Write a principle statement for the criteria listed in question
#V-8.

Answer to Question #V-11:
Your answer should be similar to the following:
Blue convertible cars with bucket seats are best.

V-12. As you can see, the principle statement allows us to be efficient in expressing principles and saves much effort and confusion. However, there are limits to the number of criteria we can handle in one such statement without creating confusion.

Question #V-12:

Suppose you wanted to state a principle that had a large number of applicable criteria. Which criteria would be of most concern to you? Which would you want to be sure to include?

Answer to question #V-12:
The most important criteria.

V-13. You would probably want to deal first with the *most* important criteria, then the less important until you got to the *least* important.

Question #V-13:

What evaluative process have you learned that would aid in the arrangement of the criteria in most, less and least categories?

Answer to question #V-13:
Ranking.

V-14. We would therefore rank all the criteria and then write the principle statement from the most important of the criteria.

Question #V-14:

In your own words, what is a principle statement?

Answer to question #V-14:
A principle statement is the combination of several criteria into a single statement, a principle.

Question #V-15:

What process would you use to ensure the inclusion of the most important criteria in the principle statement?

Answer to question #V-15:
Ranking.

Question #V-16:

Finally, the principle statement expresses and defines a_____.

Answer to question #V-16:
Principle.

SUMMARY

You have just learned that a principle can be expressed by either listing all the criteria applicable to it, or more efficiently by combining the criteria into a principle statement.

A principle statement is most easily written to include or emphasize the most important criteria by first ranking all the applicable criteria and then working from most important to least.

This is a good stopping point if you need a rest. If not, PROCEED TO LESSON VI.

LESSON VI

COMPARISON CLASS AND POINT OF VIEW

Objective: To teach what is meant by *Point of View*.
To illustrate the effects of changing the *comparison class* or *point of view*.

Question #VI-1:
You have already learned that a criterion has three parts, the a. _____ , the b. _____ and the c. _____ .

Answer to question #VI-1:
a. Comparison class, b. characteristic and c. value term.

VI-2. The parts of a criterion are derived from a rating and a description. The rating and description each has two parts.

Question #VI-2:
The parts of a rating are the _____ and the _____ .

Answer to question #VI-2:
Value object and value term.

Question #VI-3:
The parts of a description are the _____ and the

_____ .

Answer to question #VI-3:
Value object and characteristic.

Question #VI-4:
Thus the characteristic of a criterion comes from a _____
and the value term from a _____ .

Answer to question #VI-4:
Description and rating.

VI-5. You then learned that the value object in both the rating and description was very specific. A criterion has a comparison class that is usually more general than a given value object. Suppose now that a car salesman told you a sports car he was trying to sell you was a "pretty" car.

Question #VI-5:
State in writing a complete rating statement for this salesman's sports car.

Answer to question #VI-5:
Several answers are possible, one of which would be:
The sports car is pretty.

Question #VI-6:
What are the value object and value term?

Answer to question #VI-6:
The value object is the sports car. The value term is pretty.

VI-7. You remember that our model is a logical one in which the conclusion (the rating) is based upon the support offered by the major premise (the criterion) and the minor premise (the description).

Question #VI-7:
The rating, "The sports car is pretty" requires support. The support needed would be a _____ and a _____ .

Answer to question #VI-7:
Criterion and description.

VI-8. You might now ask appropriately upon what basis he rates his sports car as pretty so that you can evaluate his statement. His answer is that his sports car is pretty because it's painted purple with black polka dots.

Question #VI-8:
Supply a description and criterion for the following:
    Rating: The sports car is pretty.
    Description:
    Criterion:

Answer to question #VI-8:
    Description: The sports car is purple with black polka dots.
    Criterion: Sports cars painted purple with black polka dots are
                 pretty.

VI-9. The question now becomes whether you are willing to accept
      this support as sound. To determine this requires an evalu-
      ation of the criterion offered.
      Your evaluation of the criterion may be performed very
      quickly in your mind depending upon whether you like, dis-
      like or must decide how you feel about purple with black
      polka dot sports cars.

Question #VI-9:
    What is the comparison class in this criterion?

Answer to question #VI-9:
    Sports cars, the plural of sports car.

VI-10. Suppose you like purple with black polka dot sports cars.
      You would accept the criterion as sound, and thus would
      accept the salesman's argument and his conclusion: the rat-
      ing that his sports car is pretty.
      However, the value object *sports car* is included in several
      comparison classes. For example, all cars made in 1970, all
      passenger cars, all cars, vehicles, etc. Each of these compari-
      son classes is more general than those before it.

Question #VI-10:
    Although many people might like or accept a purple with black
polka dots colored sports car, what if we changed the comparison
class to all passenger cars? Do you think as many people would
like their passenger car painted this way?

Answer to question #VI-10:
    The author thinks not. I can't imagine many business executives
or salesmen who would want to drive such a car.

VI-11. If this is true, then the change in comparison class has re-
      sulted in the criterion "All passenger cars painted purple
      with black polka dots are pretty" which is less sound than
      the original criterion. In other words, the original criterion
      dealing with the comparison class *sports cars* tends to be
      more sound or acceptable.

Question #VI-11:
    Therefore, a change in comparison class could make a criterion
more or less_____.

Answer to question #VI-11:
Sound or acceptable.

VI-12. Notice that so far we have only considered the car from a single point of view, an aesthetic point of view based upon color. I suspect that before you'd be willing to buy the car, there are things other than color that would be of interest to you.

Question #VI-12:
Do you think it would be possible to state more than one description and criterion in support of the stated rating?

Answer to question #VI-12:
I hope you answered yes, for as you will soon see there are many possibilities.

VI-13. First let's consider descriptions. Are we concerned with the sports car's color, make, body style, year of make, motor, accessories, cost etc.? It depends upon your *point of view*. In other words, are we concerned with an aesthetic point of view, i.e., color, beauty or style; an economic point of view, cost depreciation, resale value etc.; or a performance point of view such as mileage, speed, comfort etc.?

Question #VI-13:
Suppose your point of view involved your driving comfort. What are some of the features of the car that would be of concern to you?

Answer to question #VI-13:
There are many possibilities, some of which might be seat covers, springs, shocks, arm rests, courtesy lights, radio, air conditioner, etc.

VI-14. You can readily see that an evaluation based upon support true to one point of view could lead to a conclusion (rating) quite different from that obtained with another point of view. In addition, as you saw earlier, a change in comparison class could make a criterion more or less sound.

Question #VI-14:
Therefore, before you consider the support presented by the salesman for his rating, you should first determine his_____ __ _____ and the_____ _____.

Answer to question #VI-14:
Point of view, comparison class.

SUMMARY

You have just learned that applicability and soundness of criteria and principles and, therefore, the soundness of the support for a rating, can be affected by change in the comparison class.

Furthermore, you learned that the point of view also affects which criteria are sound and useful. Different points of view sometimes affect the selection of appropriate criteria if the criteria is to provide sound support for the rating.

CRITERION TEST

Objective: The student must be able to pass the Criterion Test in writing with not less than 80% correct answers.

NOTE: Some of the blank spaces in the questions below may require more than one word. Read each question carefully and be certain you do all that is asked of you.

1. A rating has two parts, the _____ and the _____. (6 points)

2. A description also has two parts, the _____ and the _____ . (6 points)

3. A criterion has three parts, the _____ , the _____ , and the _____ . (9 points)

4. Of the three parts of a criterion, the _____ comes from the rating and the _____ from the description. (6 points)

5. First label each of the following examples as either a rating or a description. Then, draw a slash between the two parts of each statement and label the parts.

_____ a. The paper bag is pink. (3 points)
_____ b. The chocolate cake is delicious. (3 points)
_____ c. My coat is stylish. (3 points)
_____ d. The chair is scratched. (3 points)
_____ e. The book is rectangular. (3 points)
_____ f. A unicycle is fun. (3 points)
_____ g. Marriage is desirable. (3 points)

6. Using the statements below as guides, *construct* for each one a criterion statement (2 points each) and then *label* the parts of the criterion. (1 point each part)

   a. The paper bag is pink.
   b. The chocolate cake is delicious.
   c. My coat is stylish.

7. To evaluate an object as better than, worse than or the same as another object is called _____ . (3 points)

8. To evaluate an object as belonging to some category such as good or bad, desirable or undesirable, or worthwhile or worthless is called _____ . (3 points)

9. The Value-Decision Model is a logical model. Fill in the names of the parts of the Value-Decision Model that correspond to each of the following parts of a syllogism:

Syllogism   *Value-Decision Model*

Major premise   _____
Minor premise   _____
Conclusion   _____
(9 points)

10. The logic of the Value-Decision Model provides the _____ and the _____ in support of the _____ . (9 points)

11. A principle is represented by two or more _____ . (3 points)

12. Write an example of a principle statement for a good hamburger. (6 points)

4 bonus points makes a total of 100 points

●

SPECIAL NOTE

One of the important kinds of further work on value analysis is the development of programmed instruction for the tasks in value analysis, both those in Chapter 2 and those in Chapter 4. As this Yearbook goes to press, we have received word that a proposal for Title III funds to develop such programmed instruction booklets has been approved. Inquiries about progress on this project, entitled Value Analysis Capability Development Programs and under the direction of Milton Meux, should be directed to: Dr. Harold Hanley, Director of High School Education, Granite School District, 340 East 3545 South, Salt Lake City, Utah 84115.

BOOK DESIGN AND LAYOUT
by Carolyn Larson and Willadene Price

SELECTED PUBLICATIONS OF THE
NATIONAL COUNCIL FOR THE SOCIAL STUDIES
1201 SIXTEENTH ST., N.W., WASHINGTON, D.C. 20036

Yearbooks

Fortieth Yearbook (1970) *Focus on Geography: Key Concepts and Teaching Strategies*, Phillip Bacon, ed. $5.50 (490-15264); cloth $7.00 (490-15266).

Thirty-Ninth Yearbook (1969) *Social Studies Curriculum Development: Prospects and Problems*, Dorothy McClure Fraser, ed. $4.50 (490-15240); cloth $5.50 (490-15242).

Thirty-Eighth Yearbook (1968) *International Dimensions in the Social Studies*, James M. Becker and Howard D. Mehlinger, co-editors. $4.50 (490-15212); cloth $5.50 (490-15214).

Thirty-Seventh Yearbook (1967) *Effective Thinking in the Social Studies*, Jean Fair and Fannie R. Shaftel, co-editors. $4.00 (490-15188); cloth $5.00 (490-15190).

Thirty-Sixth Yearbook (1966) *Political Science in the Social Studies*, Robert E. Cleary and Donald H. Riddle, co-editors. $4.00 (490-15162); cloth $5.00 (490-15160)

Thirty-Fifth Yearbook (1965) *Evaluation in Social Studies*, Harry D. Berg, ed. $4.00 (490-15128); cloth $5.00 (490-15126)

Thirty-Fourth Yearbook (1964) *New Perspectives in World History*, Shirley H. Engle, ed. $5.00 (490-15108); cloth $6.00 (490-15106)

Thirty-Third Yearbook (1963) *Skill Development in Social Studies*, Helen McCracken Carpenter, ed. $4.00 (490-15064); cloth $5.00 (490-15062)

Bulletins

No. 45 (1971) *Concepts in the Social Studies*, Barry K. Beyer and Anthony N. Penna, eds. $2.25 (498-15248)

No. 44 (1970) *Humanities and the Social Studies*, Thomas F. Powell, ed. $3.50 (498-15246)

No. 43 (1969) *A Guide to Human Rights Education*, by Paul D. Hines and Leslie Wood. $2.25 (498-15228)

No. 42 (1969) *American History Book List for High Schools: A Selection for Supplementary Reading*, by Ralph A. Brown and Marian R. Brown. $2.50 (498-15238)

No. 41 (1968) *World Civilization Booklist: Supplementary Reading for Secondary Schools*, prepared by the World Civilization Booklist Committee of NCSS, Morris Gall and Arthur E. Soderlind, Co-Chairmen. $3.50 (498-15218)

No. 40 (1968) *Teacher-made Test Items in American History: Emphasis Junior High School*, Dana Kurfman, ed. $2.00 (498-15204)